The Visitations of Iraq to the Stations of Interlife

The Visitations of Iraq to the Stations of Interlife

Gibril Fouad Haddad

INSTITUTE FOR SPIRITUAL & CULTURAL ADVANCEMENT

First published in the US by
Institute for Spiritual & Cultural Advancement
17195 Silver Parkway #401, Fenton, MI 48430, USA
Tel: (888) 278-6624
Fax:(810) 815-0518

Email: info@sufilive.com
Web: http://www.sufilive.com
Purchase online at: http://www.isn1.net

Cover image: Mawlana al-Shaykh Muhammad Nazim Adil al-Haqqani (1340-1435/1922-2014) wearing the turban of Shaykh ʿAbd al-Qadir al-Jaylani after coming out of *khalwa* (seclusion) in the latter's *maqām* in Baghdad in mid-Shaʿbān 1386 (November 1966). Photo courtesy of Shaykh Hisham Kabbani Family Archive.

ISBN: 978-1-930409-27-9

Cataloging-in-Publication Data

Haddad, Gibril Fouad, 1960-

The Visitations of Iraq to the Stations of Interlife.
127 p. 23 cm.
1. Baghdad (Iraq) -- History. 2. Muslim Saints. 3. Islam -- Doctrine -- Barzakh. 4. Iraq -- Muslim graves. 5. Sufism -- Travel. 6. Sufism -- Principles. 7. Sunna. I. Author. II. Title.

بسم الله الرحمن الرحيم

Of the signs of the entering of the light of real belief into the servant's heart is the servant's audition of the glorifications of all creatures. The second sign is the opening of the door of wisdom to hear and understand each single glorification. The third is the free meeting with the Holy Prophet–upon him blessings and peace–and the people of *barzakh* (interlife). —Mawlana Shaykh Nazim al-Haqqani, *The Lights of Guidance from the Knowledge Oceans,* Suhba I.4.

Shaykh Nazim says... "When I entered the mosque of Sayyidina 'Abdul Qadir Jilani there was a giant man closing the door of the mosque holding it shut. He said, 'Shaykh Nazim!' 'Yes,' I answered. He said, 'I am the one assigned to be your servant during your stay here. Come with me.' I was surprised but in my heart there was no surprise because we know in tariqat everything is always arranged by the Divine Presence. I followed him as he approached the grave of the Ghawth al-A'ẓam and I gave greetings to my great-great-grandfather, Sayyidina 'Abdul Qadir Jilani. Then he took me to a room and told me, 'Every day I will serve you one bowl of lentil soup with one piece of bread.'

"I only emerged from my room for the five prayers. Otherwise I spent my whole time in that room. I was able to reach such a state that I could recite the whole Qur'an in nine hours. In addition I recited 124,000 *Dhikr* of the *Kalima* (*la ilaha illallah*) and 124,000 *salawat* (prayers on the Prophet) in addition to reading the entire *Dala'il al-Khayrat.* Added to that I was regularly reciting 313,000 'Allah Allah' every day, as well as all the prayers that were assigned to me. Vision after vision appeared to me every day. These visions took me from one state to another until I was Annihilated in the Divine Presence.

"One day I had a vision that Sayyidina 'Abdul Qadir Jilani was calling me to his grave and he was saying, 'O my son I am waiting for you at my grave. Come!' Immediately I took a shower, prayed two cycles of prayer and I walked to his grave which was only some few feet from my room. When I got there I began contemplating and I said, *as-Salamu 'alayka ya jaddī* (Peace be upon you O my grandfather). Immediately I saw him come out of the grave and stand beside me. Behind him was a Great Throne decorated with rare stones. He said to me, 'Come with me and sit with me on that throne.' We sat like a grandfather with his grandson. He was smiling and saying, 'I am happy with you. The station of your Shaykh, 'Abdullah al-Fa'iz ad-Daghestani is very high in the Naqshbandi Order. I am your grandfather and I am passing to you now, directly from me, the power that I carry as the Arch-Intercessor and I initiate you now directly into the Qadiri Order.'"

When Shaykh Nazim had finished his seclusion and was about to leave, he went to Sayyidina 'Abdul Qadir Jilani's grave to say goodbye. Sayyidina 'Abdul Qadir Jilani appeared in the flesh to him and said, "O my son. I am very happy with the states you have reached in the Naqshbandi Order. I am renewing your initiation to me through the Qadiri Order." Sayyidina 'Abdul Qadir Jilani then said, "O my grandson, I am going to give you a token of your visit." He hugged him and gave him ten coins. Those coins were from the time he was living in, not from our time. Up until today, Shaykh Nazim has kept those coins with him. Before he left, Shaykh Nazim gave the Shaykh who had served him during the seclusion, his *jubba* (cloak) as a remembrance. He told him, "I used that cloak during all of my seclusion, either as a mat to sleep on, or as a dress when praying and making dhikr. Keep it and Allah will bless you and Sayyidina Muhammad will bless you and all the Masters of this Order will bless you." The Shaykh took the cloak, kissed it, and wore it. Shaykh Nazim left Baghdad and went back to Damascus, Syria.

In 1992, when Shaykh Nazim was visiting Lahore, Pakistan, he visited the tomb of Shaykh 'Ali Hujwiri. The Shaykh of the Qadiri Order invited him to his house, and Shaykh Nazim spent the night there. At Fajr time, the Shaykh said, "O my Shaykh I kept you here tonight to show you a very precious cloak, that we have inherited 27 years ago. It was passed from one great Shaykh of the Qadiri Order to another from Baghdad, and finally it reached us. All our Shaykhs have kept it and preserved it, because it was the personal cloak of the *Ghawth* of his time. A Turkish Shaykh of the Naqshbandi Order kept seclusion in the mosque and tomb of Sayyidina 'Abdul Qadir Jilani. When that Shaykh finished his seclusion he gave the cloak as a present to a Qadiri Shaykh who had served him during his seclusion. That Qadiri Shaykh, before passing away, ordered his successors to take great care of that cloak, because if anyone wears it, he will be healed of any illness. Any seeker wearing that cloak, in his path to the Divine Presence, will be lifted easily to high states of Vision."

He opened the closet and revealed the cloak preserved in a glass case. He opened the case and took the jubba out. Shaykh Nazim was smiling. The Shaykh asked him, "What is it my Shaykh?" Shaykh Nazim said, "This brings me great happiness. This is the cloak I gave to the Qadiri Shaykh at the conclusion of my *khalwat*." When the Shaykh heard this he kissed the hand of Shaykh Nazim, asked to renew his initiation in the Qadiri Order and to take initiation in the Naqshbandi Order. Allah takes good care of his saints, wherever they go, by means of his sincere and beloved servants.

—Mawlana Shaykh Hisham Kabbani, *The Naqshbandi Sufi Way: History and Guidebook of the Saints of the Golden Chain* (pp. 397-399).

Contents

Epigraphs 7

Preamble 11

I The divine gift to human beings in the persons of the *awliyā* 13

II Allah's remembrance; the true Shaykh; the Naqshbandi guide 21

III Visit to Baghdad the City of Peace with Shaykh Jaylī al-Madanī 25

IV The life of the Friends of Allah in the *barzakh* (interlife) 29
Excerpts from Suyūṭī's *Sharḥ al-ṣudūr* (Opening of hearts) 32

V Awliya's miracles, knowledge and discretionary power after death 37

VI Fatwas on vows on behalf of a *walī*; sacrifices over his grave 47
Additional stirring hadiths and reports on the interlife 49

VII Visiting *awliyā* for Allah's pleasure: etiquette, merits, intention 56

VIII Mawlana Khālid on being with one's *murshid* at all times 61

IX The visitations of Iraq, which is the kernel of the book 67

1 'Abd al-Qādir al-Jaylānī 67
The Sufi; spiritual intuition 68
2 Ma'rūf al-Karkhī 75
3 Sarīy al-Saqaṭī 76
4 al-Junayd al-Baghdādī 77
5 Maḥmūd Aḥmad Nu'aymī 79
6 Prophet Yūsha' b. Nūn 79
7 Ibrāhīm al-Khawwāṣ 79
8 Buhlūl al-Kūfī 80
9 Salmān al-Fārisī 82
10 'Abd Allāh b. Jābir Bayāḍī 85
11 Ṭāhir b. Muḥammad Bāqir 86
12 Ḥudhayfa b. al-Yamān 86
13 Sa'īd b. Jubayr b. Hishām 87
14 Aḥmad al-Rifā'ī al-Kabīr 88
15 Sultan 'Alī Abū Aḥmad 90
16 Bahā' al-Dīn al-Rawwās 90
17 Abū Ḥanīfa al-Nu'mān 92
18 Abū Bakr al-Shiblī 93
19 Bishr al-Ḥāfī 95
20 Mūsā al-Kāẓim 97
21 Aḥmad b. Ḥanbal 98
22 'Abd Allāh b. Aḥmad 100
23 al-Ḥārith al-Muḥāsibī 100
24 Shihāb al-Dīn Suhrawardī 101
25 Aḥmad al-Ghazālī 101
26 Ḥabīb al-'Ajamī 103

X Continuation of the etiquette of visiting graves; more reference-works in addition to what was already cited 105

XI Manners in travel, dispensation and strictness 113
Manners of Mawlana Shaykh Nazim in travel 116

XII Cling to the truthful ones, study and follow a perfect Shaykh 119

Index of Quranic Verses 123
Index of Hadiths 125

Preamble

Glory to the One God Who has revealed the Qur'ān and the Sunna to His Elect and Purified Servant Muḥammad, upon him His blessings and peace, on the twin basis of which He has made the subdivisions of the sacred Law and the spiritual path branch off at the hands of the Imams and the spiritual Poles – the masters of faithfulness to their Covenant – after which He ordered love of them as an indicator of one's love for Allah and for His Messenger, and He made keeping their company and following their example an obligation. I bear witness that there is no god but the One God alone without partner, and I bear witness that our liege Lord and Master Muḥammad is His servant and Messenger, His Beloved and Elect one. O Allah! Bless Muḥammad, his Family and his Companions one and all and grant them abundant purity, safety and peace as well as their excellent followers to the Day of Recompense.

This is a brief memento of a journey to some of the oft-visited spiritual gravesites of Baghdad the City of Peace and of some other locales of Iraq – Allah protect her – during the season of the *'Urs* (spiritual marriage) of Shaykh 'Abd al-Qādir al-Jaylānī – may Allah sanctify his secret – in the month of Rabī' al-Thānī 1423, on June 18-23, 2002. The title attempts to capture the spirit of the generic Arabic terms that are used to refer to the subject, such as *ḍarīḥ* (grave-bed), *ḥaḍra* (presence), *maqām* (station, residence), *marqad* (resting-place), *mazār* (visitation), *qabr* (burial-place), *tharā* (earth), *ziyāra* (visitation). The visit took place in the company of a group of students living in blessed Damascus at the time. I mention in it a glimpse of the lives of some of those that are said to rest in those spots, their virtues and merits, and an overview of the etiquette and benefits in visiting the people of spiritual nearness and in keeping company with them in life and after death. May it be of use to the spiritual wayfarer and refresh the heart with the evocation of some of the states of some of those with whom it is believed Allah is pleased.

I have arranged the account of this journey into twelve sections: 1. The momentous divine gift to creation in the person of the Friends of Allah, their descriptions in the noble Hadiths and the fact that they are the purpose of creation. 2. The fact that the remembrance of Allah is the burnishing of the hearts, the perfect Shaykh being the most effective guide to Him, and the definition of the Naqshbandi. 3. The visit to Baghdad in Shaykh 'Abd al-Qādir b. Muḥammad b. Aḥmad b. al-Māḥī al-Jaylī's company and the merits of the City of Peace. 4. The life of the Prophets and of the *Awliyā* in their graves and what has been authored thereon. 5. Belief in the firmly-established miraculous gifts of the *Awliyā* after death and their God-given discretion. 6. Fatwas of the ulema on vowing and performing sacrifices over the grave of a *walī*. 7. The desirability of the visitation of the *Awliya*, its virtues and merits. 8. Mawlana Khālid on being with one's *murshid* at all times. 9. The central section on the Iraqi visitations which is the core of the book and its purpose. 10. Continuation of the etiquette of visiting the graves. 11. The etiquette of spiritual travel, especially for the Sultan of Awliya, Mawlana Shaykh Nazim al-Haqqani. 12. The necessity of clinging to the righteous and attaching oneself to the perfect Shaykh, which is the final chapter and the seal of musk.

Success is from Allah.

I
The divine gift to human beings in the person of the *Awliyā*

Allah has certainly lavished, in the persons of the *Awliya*, a great favor on all people on earth generally, and on the believers in particular. It is of the most momentous gifts after faith. Furthermore He made keeping close company with them and loving them something paired with belief and an indicator – or rather a precondition – of Godfearingness, since He said – exalted is He! – *O you who believe! Beware the One God and be with the truthful ones* (al-Tawba 9:119)

﴿ يَٰٓأَيُّهَا ٱلَّذِينَ ءَامَنُوا۟ ٱتَّقُوا۟ ٱللَّهَ وَكُونُوا۟ مَعَ ٱلصَّٰدِقِينَ ﴿١١٩﴾ ﴾ التوبة

and He defined the truthful and described them by saying, *of the believers are men who are true to what they covenanted with the One God. Of them is he that has fulfilled his solemn pledge, and of them is he that awaits. And they never altered with any alteration* (al-Aḥzāb 33:23).

﴿ مِّنَ ٱلْمُؤْمِنِينَ رِجَالٌ صَدَقُوا۟ مَا عَٰهَدُوا۟ ٱللَّهَ عَلَيْهِ ۖ فَمِنْهُم مَّن قَضَىٰ نَحْبَهُۥ
وَمِنْهُم مَّن يَنتَظِرُ ۖ وَمَا بَدَّلُوا۟ تَبْدِيلًا ﴿٢٣﴾ ﴾ الأحزاب

O Allah! make us firm on faith, cause us to die as people who submit and make us join the righteous.

Shaykh Yūsuf b. ʿAbd al-Hādī al-Ṣāliḥī al-Ḥanbalī (Ibn al-Mibrad) said in his book *Ṣabb al-khumūl ʿalā man waṣala adhāh ilā al-ṣāliḥīn min awliyāʾ Allah* (The downpouring of insignificance on those whose harm reaches even the righteous, i.e. the Friends of Allah), "**The *Awliya* are the supports and mainstays of the world, it is by them that the universe stands firm and it is by them that the universe is made stable.**"

فَالْأَوْلِيَاءُ أَوْتَادُ الدُّنْيَا، بِهِمْ تَثْبُتُ وَبِهِمْ تَسْتَقِرُّ

Then he said "so it is by them that their blessing is firmly-established for whoever keeps close company with them, or accompanies them, or is born to them." More, his teachers' teacher, Abū al-Faraj Ibn al-Jawzī, said before him – in the introduction of his book *Ṣifat al-ṣafwa* (Portrait of purity), "**Verily the *Awliyā* – they are the very purpose of the created universe**, because they are the luminaries of the way to Allah and the model of servanthood to Him – exalted is He! – and the manifestation of *Nor have I created the jinns and human beings but so that they would worship Me* (al-Dhāriyāt 51:56)."

إِنَّ الْأَوْلِيَاءَ هُمْ مَقْصُودُ الْكَوْنِ لأنهم مصابيح الطريق إلى الله ومثال العبودية له تعالى وظهور ﴿ وَمَا خَلَقْتُ ٱلْجِنَّ وَٱلْإِنسَ إِلَّا لِيَعْبُدُونِ ﴿٥٦﴾ ﴾ الذاريات

The Pride of beings and Light of all existents – upon him abundant blessings and greetings – listed their characteristics when he said about them in the well-known hadith: "**When they are seen, Allah is remembered**."

إِذَا رُؤُوا ذُكِرَ اللهُ

Ṭabarānī narrated it in *al-Kabīr* as did al-Bayhaqī in the *Shuʿab* (1) from Ibn Masʿūd; Ṭabarānī elsewhere from (2) ʿUbāda b. al-Ṣāmit; al-Ḥakīm al-Tirmidhī from (3) Anas and (4) Ibn ʿAbbās, as did al-Bazzār from the latter; Ibn Mājah, Aḥmad, Bukhārī in *al-Adab al-mufrad*, Abū Yaʿlā, Ṭabarānī in *al-Kabīr* and ʿAbd b. Ḥumayd from (5) Asmāʾ bint Yazīd; Bayhaqī in the *Shuʿab* from (6) Ibn ʿUmar; Abū Nuʿaym in the *Ḥilya* from (7) Saʿd b. Abī Waqqāṣ; al-Kharāʾiṭī in *Makārim al-Akhlāq* from (8) Abū Mālik al-Ashʿarī; Ibn Abī al-Dunyā in *al-Ṣamt* from (9) Abū Hurayra, and in *al-Ikhwān* and *al-Awliyāʾ* from (10) al-

Ḥasan in *mursal* (dispatched) mode; also in the latter together with al-Dūlābī in *al-Kunā wal-Asmā'* and al-Ṭabarī in his *Tafsīr* from (11) Sa'īd b. Jubayr likewise; and Ibn Abī Shayba in his *Muṣannaf* from (12) Abū al-Ḍuḥā as his own statement.

He – upon him blessings and peace – also described him in the hadith, "**The *Awliyā* are on pulpits of light.**" The hadith Master Aḥmad b. Abī Bakr b. Ismā'īl al-Būṣīrī said in *Itḥāf al-khiyarat al-mahara* that al-Ḥārith b. Muḥammad b. Abī Usāma had narrated with his chain from Abū Muslim al-Khawlānī who said, "I entered the great Mosque of Homs and behold! There were about thirty mature ones of the Companions of the Prophet – upon him the blessings and peace of Allah – and I noticed among them a young man with kohled eyes and flashing front teeth keeping silent and not speaking. Whenever the group were in doubt they would direct themselves to him and ask him. I asked the one I sat next to, 'Who is this?' He said, 'Mu'ādh b. Jabal (17BH-17 or 18/604-638 or 639)' whereupon love for him fell into my heart. I remained with them until they separated then I went back into the mosque. There was Mu'ādh b. Jabal, praying towards a column, so I prayed, then I sat and wrapped myself in my cloak, keeping silent and not speaking to him him. He kept silent and did not speak to me. Then I said, 'By Allah verily I do love you.' He said, 'For what reason do you love me?' I said, 'For Allah.' At this he grabbed my garment, pulled me gently to himself and said, 'Be happy if you speak the truth! I heard the Messenger of Allah – upon him the blessings and peace of Allah – say: '**Those who love one another for the majesty of Allah are on pulpits of light. Prophets and martyrs will long to be in their position**.'

الْمُتَحَابُّونَ فِي جَلَالِ اللهِ عَلَى مَنَابِرَ مِنْ نُورٍ، يَغْبِطُهُمُ النَّبِيُّونَ وَالشُّهَدَاءُ

"Then I went out and I met with 'Ubāda b. al-Ṣāmit. I said, 'O Abū al-Walīd! Shall I not narrate to you what Mu'ādh b. Jabal just narrated to me concerning those who love one another?' (Then he narrated it to him.) He – meaning 'Ubāda – said, 'Now I shall narrate to you what I myself heard from the Messenger of Allah –upon him the blessings and peace of Allah– who raised it all the way to the nurturing Lord – exalted is He! – Who said, "**My love has proven true for those that love one another for My sake; and My love has proven true for those that visit one another for My sake; and My love has proven true for those that give what they have for one another for My sake; and My love has proven true for those that faithfully counsel one another for My sake.**"""

حَقَّتْ مَحَبَّتِي لِلْمُتَحَابِّينَ فِيَّ، وَحَقَّتْ مَحَبَّتِي لِلْمُتَزَاوِرِينَ فِيَّ، وَحَقَّتْ مَحَبَّتِي لِلْمُتَبَاذِلِينَ فِيَّ، وَحَقَّتْ مَحَبَّتِي لِلْمُتَنَاصِحِينَ فِيَّ

Abū Ya'lā also related it with his chain to Abū Idrīs al-Khawlānī who narrated that "Mu'ādh b. Jabal grabbed me by my cloak and pulled me, asking me, 'Do you verily love me by Allah?' I said, 'By Allah I do love you for the sake of Allah.' He said, 'Receive the glad tidings! For verily I heard the Messenger of Allah – upon him the blessings and peace of Allah – say, "**Those that love one another are in the shade of His Throne on the Day there shall be no shade other than its shade.**"'

الْمُتَحَابُّونَ فِي اللهِ فِي ظِلِّ عَرْشِهِ يَوْمَ لَا ظِلَّ إِلَّا ظِلُّهُ

He said, 'Do you hear? Verily you are sitting with a people that inevitably probe the Hadith. So when you see them certainly becoming heedless then turn with longing' or he said, 'with fright to your nurturing Lord thereupon with much renewed longing or fright.'"

In another narration by Abū Ya'lā Mu'ādh said to Abū Idrīs that he heard the Messenger of Allah–upon him the blessings and peace of Allah–say, "**Those that love one another are in the shade of His Throne on the Day there shall be no shade other than its shade, the Prophets and the shahids yearning to be in their place!**"

الْمُتَحَابُّونَ فِي اللهِ فِي ظِلِّ الْعَرْشِ يَوْمَ لَا ظِلَّ إِلَّا ظِلُّهُ يَغْبِطُهُمْ بِمَكَانِهِمُ
النَّبِيُّونَ وَالشُّهَدَاءُ

Then Abū ʿUbāda said to Abū Idrīs that he heard the Messenger of Allah–upon him the blessings and peace of Allah–say, narrating from his nurturing Lord: "**My love has proven true for those that love one another for My sake; and My love has proven true for those that faithfully counsel one another for My sake; and My love has proven true for those that visit one another for My sake; and My love has proven true for those that give what they have for one another for My sake. They are on pulpits of light. The Prophets and the shahids yearn to be in their place!**"

حَقَّتْ مَحَبَّتِي لِلْمُتَحَابِّينَ فِيَّ، وَحَقَّتْ مَحَبَّتِي عَلَى الْمُتَنَاصِحِينَ فِيَّ، وَحَقَّتْ
مَحَبَّتِي عَلَى الْمُتَزَاوِرِينَ فِيَّ، وَحَقَّتْ مَحَبَّتِي عَلَى الْمُتَبَاذِلِينَ فِيَّ، عَلَى مَنَابِرَ مِنْ
نُورٍ يَغْبِطُهُمْ بِمَكَانِهِمُ النَّبِيُّونَ وِالشُّهَدَاءُ

The hadith Master al-Būṣīrī said, "Mālik narrated it with a sound chain, also Ibn Ḥibbān in his *Ṣaḥīḥ* in complete form, also al-Tirmidhī, the hadith of Muʿādh only, and he said it was fair and sound." He added that Abū Yaʿlā also narrated from Abū Hurayra that the Messenger of Allah – upon him the blessings and peace of Allah – said, "**Verily there are, of the servants of Allah, certain servants about whom the Prophets and the shahids yearn to be in their place**." They asked, "Who are they? Perhaps we can love them!" He said, "**A people who loved one another for the light of Allah, without blood relation and without lineage. Their faces are light, they are on pulpits of light, they do not fear when people fear, they do not grow sad when people grow sad. Then he recited, *Behold! Verily the friends of the One God, there is no fear for them, nor shall they grieve*** (Yūnus 10:62)."

إِنَّ مِنْ عِبَادِ اللهِ عِبَاداً يَغْبِطُهُمُ الأَنْبِيَاءُ وَالشُّهَدَاءُ. قيل: من هم لعلّنا نُحبّهم؟ قال: قَوْمٌ تَحَابُّوا بِنُورِ اللهِ عَزَّ وَجَلَّ مِنْ غَيْرِ أَرْحَامٍ وَلَا أَنْسَابٍ، وُجُوهُهُمْ نُورٌ، عَلَى مَنَابِرَ مِنْ نُورٍ، لَا يَخَافُونَ إِذَا خَافَ النَّاسُ، وَلَا يَحْزَنُونَ إِذَا حَزِنَ النَّاسُ. ثُمَّ قَرَأَ: ﴿أَلَآ إِنَّ أَوۡلِيَآءَ ٱللَّهِ لَا خَوۡفٌ عَلَيۡهِمۡ وَلَا هُمۡ يَحۡزَنُونَ ٦٢﴾

Al-Būṣīrī further cited Ibn Abī Usāma with his chain to Abū Mālik al-Ashʿarī who related that the Prophet – upon him the blessings and peace of Allah – one day, finished his prayer then turned to face the people and said: "**People! Listen to this, understand it, and know it. Allah has servants who are neither Prophets nor martyrs and whom the Prophets and martyrs yearn to resemble due to their seat and proximity in relation to Allah**." One of the desert Arabs who came from among the most isolated of people twisted his hand at the Prophet and said: "Messenger of Allah! People from humankind who are neither Prophets nor martyrs and yet the Prophets and the martyrs yearn to be like them due to their seat and proximity in relation to Allah? Describe them for us!" The face of the Prophet showed delight at the question and he said: "**They are strangers from here and there. They frequent this tribe or that without belonging to any of them. They do not have family connections with each other. They love one another for the sake of Allah. They are of pure intent towards one another. On the Day of Resurrection Allah shall place for them pedestals of light upon which He shall seat them, and He will turn their faces and clothes into light. On the Day of Resurrection the people will be terrified, but not those ones. They are *the Friends of Allah upon whom fear comes not, nor do they grieve*** (10:62)."

يَا أَيُّهَا النَّاسُ، اِسْمَعُوا واعْقِلُوا وَاعْلَمُوا أَنَّ للهِ عَزَّ وَجَلَّ عِبَاداً لَيْسُوا بِأَنْبِيَاءَ وَلَا شُهَدَاءَ، يَغْبِطُهُمُ النَّبِيُّونَ وَالشُّهَدَاءُ عَلَى مَنَازِلِهِمْ وَقُرْبِهِمْ مِنَ اللهِ. هُمْ نَاسٌ مِنْ أَفْنَاءِ النَّاسِ، وَنَوَازِعِ الْقَبَائِلِ، لَمْ تَصِلْ بَيْنَهُمْ أَرْحَامٌ مُتَقَارِبَةٌ، تَحَابُّوا فِي اللهِ وَتَصَافَوا، يَضَعُ اللهُ لَهُمْ يَوْمَ الْقِيَامَةِ مَنَابِرَ مِنْ نُورٍ فَيُجْلِسُهُمْ عَلَيْهَا، فَيَجْعَلُ وُجُوهَهُمْ نُوراً، وَثِيَابَهُمْ نُوراً،

يَفْزَعُ النَّاسُ يَوْمَ الْقِيَامَةِ وَلَا يَفْزَعُونَ، وَهُمْ أَوْلِيَاءُ اللهِ،

﴿لَا خَوْفٌ عَلَيْهِمْ وَلَا هُمْ يَحْزَنُونَ﴾

Abū Ya'lā al-Mawṣilī narrated it, as did Aḥmad b. Ḥanbal in his *Musnad*, from Abū Mālik; also al-Ḥākim with a different chain from Ibn 'Umar, and he said it had a sound chain. Something similar is also narrated from 'Umar b. al-Khaṭṭāb – Allah be well-pleased with him – from the Prophet – upon him the blessings and peace of Allah – in Abū Dāwūd's *Sunan*. Ya'qūb b. Sufyān al-Fasawī also narrated in *al-Ma'rifa wal-Tārīkh* from 'Abd Allāh b. 'Amr b. al-'Āṣ, that the Prophet – upon him the blessings and peace of Allah – said, "**Blessed are the strangers!**" It was asked: "Who are they, Messenger of Allah?" He said: "**Righteous people who are few among many evil people; those who disobey them outnumber those who obey them.**"

طُوبَى لِلْغُرَبَاءِ. نَاسٌ صَالِحُونَ قَلِيلٌ فِي نَاسٍ سُوءٍ كَثِيرٍ، مَنْ يَعْصِيهِمْ أَكْثَرُ مِمَّنْ يُطِيعُهُمْ

Ibn 'Amr continued, "One day we were with him when the sun was rising and he said: '**A people will come to Allah on the Day of Resurrection, their light like that of the sun.**' Abū Bakr asked, 'Are we those people, Messenger of Allah?' He said: 'No, and you will have immense goodness; but **these are the poor emigrants. Bad things are averted through them. Each of them dies with his worldly need unfulfilled** [lit. "with his need stuck in his chest"]. **They will be resurrected from the four corners of the world.**'"

يَأْتِي اللهَ عَزَّ وَجَلَّ فِي يَوْمِ الْقِيَامَةِ قَوْمٌ نُوْرُهُمْ كَالشَّمْسِ. فقال أبو بكر: نَحْنُ هُمْ يَا رَسُولَ اللهِ؟ قال: لَا، وَلَكُمْ خَيْرٌ كَثِيرٌ، وَلَكِنَّهُمْ فُقَرَاءُ الْمُهَاجِرِينَ. تُتَّقَى بِهِمُ الْمَكَارِهُ، يَمُوتُ أَحَدُهُمْ وَحَاجَتُهُ فِي صَدْرِهِ. يُحْشَرُونَ مِنْ أَقْطَارِ الْأَرْضِ

II
The remembrance of Allah, the perfect Shaykh and the qualities of the Naqshbandi spiritual guide

"The remembrance of Allah is the polish of the hearts." Therefore, just as the *walī* is never beheld by any possessor of a heart but Allah is remembered, likewise the one in quest of the purification of the heart and the growth of the soul, when he or she sits with the *walī* and love him for the sake of Allah, they have reached their goal. So then it is imperative to visit the righteous, to spend time with them, to frequent them for the same reason that it is obligatory to purely dedicate one's intention in acts of worship and transactions. That is why the Proof of Islam, Imam al-Ghazālī, stipulated that it is compulsory to find and keep a spiritual guide, and before him Abū Yazīd al-Bisṭāmī said, "Whoever has no shaykh, the devil is his shaykh." For he falls into self-admiration and becomes content to have his ego as his spiritual director. He has set up his own mortal enemy as a sentinel over the forts of his jihad in the way of Allah and has gone against the statement of the Infallible one – upon him and his Family and Companions the blessings and peace of Allah – that "**A person follows the faith-system of their friend; therefore let each of you look well who they have as their friend!**" It is narrated from Abū Hurayra by Abū Dāwūd and al-Tirmidhī, and the latter declared it fair.

الرَّجُلُ عَلَى دِينِ خَلِيلِهِ فَلْيَنْظُرْ أَحَدُكُمْ مَنْ يُخَالِلُ

Thus the perfect Shaykh is the curber of the ego and its expert trainer, the unfailing guide to Allah and His Messenger with respect to correct creed, worship and behavior. That is why our liege Lord Jabra'īl – upon him peace – defined the faith-system as *īmān*, *islām* and *iḥsān* in the well-known hadith from our liege lord 'Umar in the two *Ṣaḥīḥ*s. Thus did the early Masters define *taṣawwuf*. Some defined it as pure monotheism; some as the shunning of prohibited things and the performance of obligations and Sunna acts in the most perfect way; some as doing with little, keeping silent and staying hungry; and some as treating others in the most excellent manner, serving them and enduring the harm they do to you for the sake of Allah. Success is from Allah, and the one who is connected is not like the one who is disconnected. The Prophet – upon him the blessings and peace of Allah – said, "**You must keep with the congregation. Beware of parting with them! For the devil is with the solitary one whereas he keeps farther from the two. Whoever wants to bask in Paradise, let him keep to the congregation.**"

عَلَيْكُمْ بِالْجَمَاعَةِ وَإِيَّاكُمْ وَالْفُرْقَةَ، فَإِنَّ الشَّيْطَانَ مَعَ الْوَاحِدِ؛ وَهُوَ مِنَ الاِثْنَيْنِ أَبْعَدُ؛ مَنْ أَرَادَ بُحْبُوحَةَ الْجَنَّةِ فَلْيَلْزَمِ الْجَمَاعَةَ

It is narrated in the *Sunan*. Mawlana Shaykh Muhammad Nazim al-Haqqani – may Allah sanctify his secret – said that the perfect spiritual guide is rarer than the purest gold but whoever is earnest shall find. Thereafter, the one that is connected with the lofty presence will surely direct the sincere seeker whom Allah led to him. Shaykh Muḥyī al-Dīn Ibn ʿArabī said, "and whoever dies on the way is recorded among those that have arrived," so one must keep journeying.

Blessings then to whoever has reached him and has reached Mawlana Shaykh Muhammad Hisham Kabbani the caliph of Mawlana Shaykh Nazim al-Haqqani with absolute certainty and his outward and inward inheritor, the teacher of beautiful opinion about Allah and the one that raised high the standard of the Prophet – upon him the blessings and peace of Allah – east and west, especially in the countries of Europe, north America and southeast Asia, whereby their followers have filled the four corners of the world, revived the practice of the faith, taught the obligations and the Sunnas, recited the Magnificent Book of Allah, reminded others and admonished them, calling them in the most excellent ways and exemplary behavior, wearing the turban and the robe and the beard, carrying the staff in the manner of the righteous, distributing the pearl and coral of spiritual reminders of the hereafter and precious discourse to every questioner and witness. For neither was ever stingy of what they were given of the knowledge of Allah and of His Messenger. And all is by the help of Allah then by the blessing of the Master of creatures – upon him the blessings and peace of Allah – and the spiritual extensions of the Khwajagan Masters. Thus whoever sees them remembers Allah and, likewise, whoever hears them, keeps company with them, reads about them, takes them as his guardians and loves them.

The Imam of the Way and the Arch-Helper of creatures Shah Naqshband Muḥammad b. Muḥammad b. Muḥammad Bahā' al-Dīn al-Uwaysī al-Bukhārī – may Allah sanctify his secret – said, "The spiritual director has to know the states of his seeker in the three historic times – the past, the future and the present – so that it will be possible for him to raise and nurture him; and the wayfarer must be, upon meeting with one of those that are beloved to Allah, vigilantly watchful of his own state. Then let him weigh the time of his *suḥba* (companionship) and compare it to that of his previous time. If he finds that he has proceeded, with respect to his state, from deficiency towards perfection, then – in the terms of his statement, 'You have found the right way (*aṣabta*) so stick to it! (*fa-lzam*)' [in reference to the Prophetic Hadith, '**How are you this morning O Ḥāritha?**' which is also narrated with the word '**You have reached recognition so stick to it** (*'arafta fa-ⁱlzam*)'], then let him make his accompaniment of this beloved rare one a personal categorical obligation binding on himself!" He also said – may Allah sanctify his secret – "Whoever has inclined towards us or has affiliated himself or herself to our love – whether they are near or far – we must notice his affiliation every day and night and we must extend to him support from the wellspring of the source of compassion and nurture and continuous support if he or she preserves his or her states, keeping the path of support clean and free of the blemishes of excessive worldly attachments and their dirtiness."

The Exalted Lord of all has certainly lavished favor on the writer of these lines, indeed the greatest favor after belief, consisting in companionship with the seal of *wilāya*, the standard-bearer of the perfect ones and the remnant of the lofty masters of the spiritual path successively known as the Muhammadan, Siddiqi, Uwaysi, Tayfuri, Ghujduwani, Khwajagani, Naqshbandi, Mujaddidi, Khalidi, Daghistani path, the Sultan of the Friends of Allah, of Jaylānī Ḥasanī-Ḥusaynī descent on his father's side and of Mevlevi Bakrī descent on his mother's side, Mawlana Shaykh Muhammad Nazim Adil, son of Sayyid Ahmad, son of Sayyid Hasan Yashīl al-Ṣāliḥī al-Qubruṣī al-Ḥaqqānī (1341-1435/1922-2014) and companionship with his successor and son-in-law whom he named *al-Quṭb al-mutaṣarrif* (the Spiritual Pole of discretion), Mawlana Shaykh Muhammad Hisham the son of al-Hajj Muhammad Salim Kabbani al-Ḥusaynī al-Naqshbandī al-Ḥaqqāni al-Lubnānī al-Shāfiʿī (b. on al-Aḥad 14 Ṣafar 1364 / 28 January 1945), also known as *Madad al-Ḥaqq* (the Help from the All-True), both of them true successors of Sultan al-Awliya' Mawlana Shaykh Abdullah Fa'iz al-Daghistani – may Allah sanctify their secret, and may He benefit us and the Umma of our liege Lord Muḥammad, upon him and his Family and Companions blessings and peace, with them.

Allah Most High had already bestowed from before as well, of bestowals and kindnesses that which only He may count – and He is the Owner of glorification, praise and thanks, the Giver of Godfearingness and the Possessor of all forgiveness, *the Forgiver of the sin and the Accepter of repenting, the Severe in retribution, the Repriever! There is no god but He. Unto Him is the destination* (al-Mu'min / Ghāfir 40:3).

﴿ غَافِرِ ٱلذَّنۢبِ وَقَابِلِ ٱلتَّوۡبِ شَدِيدِ ٱلۡعِقَابِ ذِي ٱلطَّوۡلِۖ لَآ إِلَٰهَ إِلَّا هُوَۖ إِلَيۡهِ
ٱلۡمَصِيرُ ﴿٣﴾ ﴾ غافر

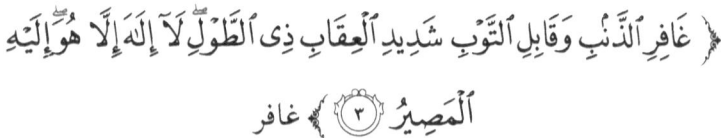

III

Visit to Baghdad the City of Peace together with Shaykh ʿAbd al-Qādir b. Muḥammad b. Aḥmad b. al-Māḥī al-Jaylī

Of the Lordly extensions of mercy and the abundant allowances and miraculous gifts of the exalted divine presence in our two Masters—Mawlana Shaykh Nazim and Mawlana Shaykh Hisham—is companionship of the pious—the Shaykhs of sacred knowledge and of the spiritual path—and the meeting with the people of Allah at their doorsteps and in their gatherings. Shah Naqshband said, "**Our path is companionship, and goodness is in collectedness.**" From the beginning of my quest I had asked permission of Mawlana Shaykh Hisham to go to the gatherings of goodness. He gave me permission on condition that I observe the Sunna of the turban. Five years later he interceded with Sultan al-Awliyāʾ Mawlana Shaykh Nazim for me to take up residence in his Damascus house on Mount Qasyūn. Five more years later I met Mawlana's younger cousin the noble Sharif, Shaykh ʿAbd al-Qādir ibn Māḥī al-Jaylī al-Madanī (b. 1960) during his visit to Damascus, from where he took me with him to the visit of Baghdad the City of Peace–may Allah keep her secure. We went in the season of the *ʿurs* (anniversary of the soul's divine meeting) of the Ghawth al-Aʿẓam, Sultan al-Awliyāʾ Shaykh ʿAbd al-Qādir al-Jaylānī in the month of Rabīʿ al-Thānī 1423, corresponding to the 18th to the 23rd of June 2002. That was where, Mawlana Shaykh Nazim had said, "Mawlana Shaykh ʿAbd Allah ordered me to enter seclusion in the *maqām* of our liege lord ʿAbd al-Qadir al-Jaylani for 40 days. I met with Sayyidi Shaykh ʿAbd al-Qadir spiritually and he spoke to me a suhba that has been engraved in my heart" (Suhba I.26 in Mawlana's *The Lights of Guidance*). That seclusion took place from the first of Rajab to the tenth of Shaʿbān 1386 (mid-October to late November 1966), at the culmination of Mawlana's 46th year.

Shaykh ʿAbd al-Qādir al-Jaylī is the son of the supercentenarian Knower of Allah, Muḥammad b. Aḥmad b. al-Māḥī b. Uṣūl, nicknamed Wadd al-Bukhārī, al-Madanī al-Jaylī al-Ḥusaynī al-Sūdānī, famed as Abūnā (our father) al-Shaykh, born between the years 1864-1867 in the town of Daym al-Jaʿliyyīn in the state of Sennār in Sudan. He died in the year 2000 in Medina, aged 140 years. May Allah have mercy on him. Shaykh ʿAbd al-Qādir al-Jaylī took the Qadiri path from Dr. Bakr b. ʿAbd al-Razzāq al-Sāmarrāʾī al-Baghdādī (d. 2021) the imam and preacher of the Mosque of Shaykh ʿAbd al-Qādir al-Jaylānī and author of the book *Qawāʿid al-akhlāq fil-taṣawwuf al-islāmī* (The rules of high character in Islamic *taṣawwuf*) and from our liege lord Shaykh Muḥammad ʿAbd al-Qādir Maʿīnī al-Ḥimṣī, from our liege lord Shaykh Muḥammad b. Aḥmad b. al-Māḥī, from Shaykh ʿAbd al-Bāqī b. ʿUmar b. Aḥmad al-Mukāshifī with his chain to Shaykh ʿAbd al-Qādir al-Jaylānī. Shaykh al-Jaylī also took the Naqshbandi path from Shaykh Maḥmūd Aḥmad al-Nuʿaymī al-Baghdādī and Shaykh Muḥammad ʿAbd al-Qādir Maʿīnī al-Ḥimṣī al-Ḥalabī – may Allah sanctify their secrets one and all.

In thankfulness I recorded the memento of this journey in a few quires written in Arabic which I entitled *al-Ziyārāt al-ʿirāqiyya ilā al-maqāmāt al-barzakhiyya wa-nukhbat al-ādāb li-man qaṣada al-aʿtāb* (The visitations of Iraq to the stations of interlife and the best of etiquettes for the seekers of the spiritual thresholds). Twenty-two years later I am grateful to be able to bring out its English version.

May Allah ever bless our spiritual guides and thank them.

The greatness of Iraq and its capital Baghdad, the City of Peace

Abū Bakr Aḥmad b. ʿAlī al-Khaṭīb al-Baghdādī narrated in his *Tārīkh Baghdād madīnat al-salām* from Shuʿba, from both Abū Bakr b. ʿAyyāsh and Imam al-Shāfiʿī–Allah have mercy on all of them–the statement, "Whoever has not seen Baghdad has not seen the world;" and from Abū Muʿāwiya, "Baghdad is an abode of this world and of the hereafter;" and from al-Shāfiʿī, "I never entered a country but I counted it as a journey except for Baghdad; for when I entered it I counted it as a home." It was also said, "the earth is all a desert whose inhabited part is Baghdad." Hārūn al-Rashīd reportedly said of it, "It is the *sikka* (mint) for the whole world." Dhū al-Nūn al-Miṣrī said, "Whoever wants to learn discretion and brilliance, let him study the water-carriers in Baghdad." Sulaymān b. Mūsā said, "If a man's knowledge is of the Hijaz and his character is of Iraq and his obedience is of Syro-Palestine then he has become perfect. Abū al-Ḥusayn Aḥmad b. Jaʿfar b. al-Munādī listed among its virtues "noble characters, well-pleasing dispositions, copious sweet water, abundant pulpy fruit, beautiful states, expertise in every craft, resource for every need, protection against the emergence of detestable innovations, just pride in the multitude of ulema, students, jurists, students of jurisprudence, foremost leaders of the theologians, masters of arithmetics, grammarians, top poets, chroniclers, genealogists and authorities in all the different disciplines."

Iraq is indeed of the great storehouses of Allah whose reality only He truly knows. Al-Khaṭīb said, "And on top of this [immense wealth] it is always victorious and marked with happiness. Every time the enemies of Islam think they have achieved the annihilation of its people Allah overthrows them and hurls them down face first, and their power is uprooted in a way that lies beyond the devising of all creatures, *as a bounty from the One God and a blessing; and the One God is the bestower of immense bounty.*" It suffices it for honor that countless Companions of the Prophet have moved there and made it their home, and the elite of the Successors and the Imams of *tafsīr*, Hadith, fiqh, *taṣawwuf* and theology – the best of ages as spoken by the Master of creatures–upon him the blessings and peace of Allah–who described its Euphrates as one of the rivers of Paradise. Moreover it is carpeted with the *maqāms* (oft-visited spiritual gravesites), especially those of the Poles of the Sufi arch-masters. So Iraq in general and Baghdad in particular are of the major spiritual capitals and the attested stations of the hereafter.

IV
The life of the Friends of Allah in the *barzakh* (interlife)

The Friends of Allah are alive in their graves in keeping with their spiritual Prophetic inheritorship including the knowledge of Allah and its effect on their essences by His permission, a God-given effect and a pure bounty from Him–exalted is He–in life and after death, due to the effect that the purity of their inward selves and their spirits has over their outward persons and their bodies, consisting in an angelic transparent luminosity the spiritual masters expressed as the shedding of the attributes of humanness, as in the poet's words,

when the brook becomes still, in a state of purity,
and is kept from being stirred up by the breeze,
you may see in it the sky without any doubt.
Likewise the sun appears, likewise the stars,
likewise the faces of those of the loftiest heights,
in whose pureness is seen the All-Magnificent.

Under this very chapter are subsumed the words of the Prophetic Companions in which they described the greatest Beloved as a light walking on the face of the earth, as in the poetry and reports of Ḥassān b. Thābit, al-ʿAbbās b. ʿAbd al-Muṭṭalib, Kaʿb b. Zuhayr, ʿUmar b. al-Khaṭṭāb, ʿAtika bint ʿAbd al-Muṭṭalib, al-Rubayyiʿ bint Muʿawwidh, Abū Hurayra, Anas, Ṭāriq b. ʿAbd Allāh al-Muḥāribī, al-ʿIrbāḍ b. Sāriya, Abū Umāma, ʿUtba b. ʿAbd al-Sulamī and others – may Allah be well-pleased with all of them. They are documented in *The Muhammadan Light in the Qur'ān, Sunna and Companion-Reports.* The noble Prophets and Messengers and their inheritors among the Friends of Allah are all drops from the ocean of the light of the Seal of Prophets – upon him and them blessings and peace.

And every sign the noble Messengers have brought
was only a link to them out of his very own light.
For he is a bountiful sun whose planets they all are,
manifesting its light in pitch darkness for all people.

O Allah! bless and grant him abundant purity, safety and peace.

Imam al-Bayhaqī mentioned in his book, *The life of Prophets in their graves*, among the well-known evidentiary texts which no one denies but the bankrupt, I. the Prophetic hadith, "**The Prophets are alive in their graves, praying,**"

الأَنْبِيَاءُ أَحْيَاءٌ فِي قُبُورِهِمْ يُصَلُّونَ

narrated from Anas by Abū Yaʿlā in his *Musnad* with a chain of trust-worthy narrators. It was declared sound by the Arch-master Ibn Ḥajar in *Fatḥ al-Bārī*, al-Zurqānī in *Sharḥ al-Muwaṭṭaʾ* and al-Suyūṭī in *Inbāʾ al-adhkiyāʾ bi-ḥayāt al-Anbiyāʾ* (The informing of the intelligent of the lives of the Prophets [in their graves]); II. the Prophetic hadith, "**I passed by Mūsā on the night I was taken on a night journey, at the red dune, as he was standing, praying in his grave,**"

أَتَيْتُ - وفي رواية - مَرَرْتُ عَلَى مُوسَى لَيْلَةَ أُسْرِيَ بِي عِنْدَ الْكَثِيبِ الأَحْمَرِ وَهُوَ قَائِمٌ يُصَلِّي فِي قَبْرِهِ

narrated from Anas by Aḥmad, al-Nasāʾī, Muslim, Abū Yaʿlā, Ibn Abī Shayba, ʿAbd b. Ḥumayd and Ibn Khuzayma and his student Ibn Ḥibbān in their respective *Ṣaḥīḥs*; and III. the Prophetic hadith, "**Verily Allah has made it prohibited for the earth to consume the bodies ot the Prophets**" – upon them peace,

إِنَّ اللهَ عَزَّ وَجَلَّ قَدْ حَرَّمَ عَلَى الأَرْضِ أَنْ تَأْكُلَ أَجْسَادَ الأَنْبِيَاءِ عَلَيْهِمُ السَّلامُ

narrated from (i) Aws b. Aws by Aḥmad, al-Dārimī, al-Nasā'ī, Abū Dāwūd, Ibn Mājah, Ibn Khuzayma, Ibn Ḥibbān, al-Ṭabarānī in *al-Kabīr* and al-Ḥākim who rated it *ṣaḥīḥ* per the criterion of Muslim; and (ii) Abū al-Dardā' by Ibn Mājah, and al-Būṣīrī rated it *ṣaḥīḥ* in *Miṣbāḥ al-zujāja* and there is in it the addition "**so the Prophet of Allah is living and provided for**."

فَنَبِيُّ اللهِ حَيٌّ يُرْزَقُ

Allah Most High said in regard to the interlife of the shahids, *and do not say, about those who are killed in the way of the One God, "Dead;" rather "Alive;" but you do not perceive* (al-Baqara 2:154).

﴿وَلَا تَقُولُوا۟ لِمَن يُقْتَلُ فِى سَبِيلِ ٱللَّهِ أَمْوَٰتٌۢ ۚ بَلْ أَحْيَآءٌ وَلَٰكِن لَّا تَشْعُرُونَ ﴿١٥٤﴾﴾ البقرة

He also said, *and never count those who were killed in the way of the One God as dead; rather alive with their nurturing Lord, receiving provision* (Āl 'Imrān 3:169).

﴿وَلَا تَحْسَبَنَّ ٱلَّذِينَ قُتِلُوا۟ فِى سَبِيلِ ٱللَّهِ أَمْوَٰتًۢا ۚ بَلْ أَحْيَآءٌ عِندَ رَبِّهِمْ يُرْزَقُونَ ﴿١٦٩﴾﴾

آل عمران

It was also established of some of the shahids among the Companions that they never decomposed in their graves, such as 'Umar b. al-Khaṭṭāb, 'Amr b. al-Jamūḥ al-Anṣārī al-Sulamī, 'Abd Allāh b. 'Amr al-Anṣārī al-Sulamī, and 'Abd Allāh b. Ḥarām al-Anṣārī the father of Jābir –Allah be well-pleased with them all! It was also established to be true about some of the shahids that died in the *fatra* (interval period) between our liege Lord ʿĪsā and our liege Lord Muḥammad – upon them blessings and peace – as narrated by al-Tirmidhī in the story of *the makers of the ditch* (al-Burūj 85:4). Imam al-Qurṭubī mentioned all of the above in his book *al-Tadhkira fī aḥwāl al-mawtā wal-ākhira* (Memento of the states of the dead and the hereafter). And the Prophets and the Most-truthful are above them in level.

Among the references with respect to the proof-texts on the life of the Friends of Allah in their graves is Ibn Abī al-Dunyā's *Kitāb al-qubūr* (The book of the graves); his *Kitāb man ʿāsha baʿda al-mawt* (Those that lived after death); al-Bayhaqī's abovementioned *Ḥayāt al-Anbiyāʾ*; his book *al-Baʿth wal-nushūr* (Resurrection and the rising); ʿAbd al-Ḥaqq al-Ishbīlī's *al-ʿĀqiba* (The hereafter); Qurṭubī's abovementioned *al-Tadhkira*; Ibn Rajab's book *Ahwāl al-qubūr wa-aḥwāl ahlihā ilā al-nushūr* (The horrors of the graves and the states of their dwellers until the rising of the dead); Suyūṭī's *Sharḥ al-ṣudūr* (The expanding of the breasts); his book *Bushrā al-kaʾīb bi-liqāʾ al-Ḥabīb* (The glad tidings for the distressed in the meeting with the Beloved); and his book *al-Fawz al-ʿaẓīm bi-liqāʾ al-Karīm* (The immense triumph in the meeting with All-Munificent); and others.

Some of what al-Suyūṭī mentioned in his book *Sharḥ al-ṣudūr*

Imam al-Suyūṭī – Allah have mercy on him – said in *Sharḥ al-Ṣudūr*: "[The ascetic Shāfiʿī qadi, jurist, legal theorist, preacher, astronomer and author of many books, Abū al-Maʿalī ʿAzīzī b. ʿAbd al-Malik b. Manṣūr al-Azjī al-Jaylānī, known as] Shaydhala (d. 494/1101) said in the book *al-Burhān fī ʿulūm al-Qurʾān* [= *al-Burhān fī mushkilāt al-Qurʾān* (The demonstration concerning the difficulties of the Qurʾān)], 'So if it asked about the saying of Allah, *and never count those who were killed in the way of the One God as dead; rather alive*, etc. (Āl ʿImrān 3:169),

﴿ وَلَا تَحْسَبَنَّ ٱلَّذِينَ قُتِلُوا۟ فِى سَبِيلِ ٱللَّهِ أَمْوَٰتًۢا ۚ بَلْ أَحْيَآءٌ عِندَ رَبِّهِمْ يُرْزَقُونَ ﴿١٦٩﴾ ﴾

آل عمران

we say that it is possible that Allah gives them back life in their graves and four their souls to reside in some part of their bodies, the whole body experiencing bliss and pleasure because of that part, just as the whole body of the one living in the world may feel coldness or heat that might be in some part of his body. It was also said that what is meant is that their bodies do not decompose in their graves and their connections are not severed, so they are as living in their graves.' Abū Ḥayyān said in his Quranic commentary on that verse, 'People differed concerning this life. Some said its meaning is the perdurance of their souls without their bodies, because we may witness the latter's decomposition and disappearance. Others said that the shahid is alive body and soul, which is not invalidated by our lack of perception of it, for we see them in the guise of the dead while they are living, just as Allah has said, *and you shall see the mountains, reckoning them to be fixed whereas they are passing the way clouds pass* (Naml 27:88),

﴿ وَتَرَى ٱلْجِبَالَ تَحْسَبُهَا جَامِدَةً وَهِىَ تَمُرُّ مَرَّ ٱلسَّحَابِ ﴾ النمل

and just as the sleeper might be seen in a certain form while he himself sees, in his dream, that which delights him or that by which he feels pain.'

"I [= al-Suyūṭī] say, this is why He said – exalted is He – *rather 'Alive;' but you do not perceive* (al-Baqara 2:154),

﴿ بَلْ أَحْيَآءٌ وَلَٰكِن لَّا تَشْعُرُونَ ﴾ البقرة

whereby He gave notification to the believers of the fact that they cannot perceive this life through eyewitnessing and sensory perception. It is in this way that the shahid is marked off from others. For if what was meant were only the life of the spirit, he would be no different from others, since all the deceased share that with him and because the entirety of the believers know that all spirits live on. Thus His statement *but you do not perceive* would make no sense. Now Allah might grant His Friends a disclosure whereby they witness that. Suhaylī related in *Dalā'il al-Nubuwwa* from one of the Companions that he was digging in a certain spot, whereupon an opening was revealed and – behold! – there was someone sitting on a dais with a volume of the Qur'ān opened before him in which he was reading, and before him there was a green grove. That was in Uḥud, and he realized that he was one of the shahids because he saw a cut on the side of his face. Abū Ḥayyān also mentioned that. Similar to this is what al-Yāfi'ī related in *Rawḍ al-rayyāḥīn* from one of the righteous that he said, 'I dug out a grave for a man who was one of the staunch worshippers and laid him in the side-niche. As I was adjusting the side-niche a brick from the adjacent grave's side-niche fell off so I looked, and – behold! – there was an old man sitting in the grave wearing white clothes, moving and making a rustling sound, before his lap a volume of the Qur'ān made of gold in which he was reading. He raised his head towards me and said to me, "Has the Resurrection started – may Allah grant you mercy?" I said no. He said, "Put back the brick in its place – may Allah grant you health." So I put it back.'

"Al-Yāfi'ī also said, 'One of the trustworthy gravediggers narrated to us that he once dug out a grave, whereupon he came upon a human being sitting therein on a dais with a volume of the Qur'ān in his hand in which he was reading, and beneath him there was river running, so he fainted and was pulled out of the grave. No one knew what had happened to him and he did not come to until the third day.' He also related from Shaykh Najm al-Dīn al-Aṣbahānī that the latter was present at a certain man's burial, after which the *mulaqqin* (prompter) sat down and started to prompt him [= the deceased]. The deceased was then heard saying, 'Do you not wonder how the dead can be prompting the living?'" What the voice said is like what Muwaffaq Ibn Abī al-Ḥaram al-Shāri'ī (d. 615/1218) said in the exordium to his book *Murshid al-zuwwār ilā qubūr al-abrār*: "The graves of the pious are staunch houses. It is where the Sultan's close circle come for their direst woes. You will see those in need go around them to find one with the greatest standing and sanctity, so they ask help there for their intercession. The speech of states responds and speaks, so do not look at the desolation of their appearances: within, they are groves wherein delight the soul of the righteous. Stand at their graves with manners, feel shy and say, 'O living ones! Ask mercy upon a dead one. O wealthy ones! Show munificence to a bankrupt one.' And weep over the loss of your years of life in vain pursuits, and feel regret." End of al-Shāri'ī's words.

Al-Suyūṭī went on: "Yāfi'ī also related from al-Muḥibb al-Ṭabarī – one of the Imams of the Shāfi'īs, and he is the commentator of [al-Shīrāzī's] *al-Tanbīh* [in fiqh], 'I once was with Shaykh Ismā'īl al-Ḥaḍramī in the cemetery in Zabīd, whereupon the latter said to me, "Tell me, O Muḥibb! Do you believe in the speaking of the dead?" I said yes. He said, "Verily the dweller of this grave is presently saying to me that he is part of the stuff of Paradise!"'"

V
Belief in the firmly-established miraculous gifts of the *Awliyā* after death, their God-given knowledge and discretionary power

Shaykh ʿAbd al-Ghanī al-Nābulusī said in *Jamʿ al-asrār fī manʿi al-ashrār ʿani al-ṭaʿni fīl-Ṣūfiyyat al-akhyār* (The compendium of secrets in preventing the evildoers from casting aspersions against the Sufis, the elite) that the erudite Imam Muḥammad al-Shawbarī al-Miṣrī said in substance, "The *karāmāt* (miraculous gifts) of the *Awliyā* are firmly-established. **Their *taṣarruf* (discretionary power) does not cease by virtue of death** and *tawassul* (using intermediacy) through them to Allah—like *istighātha* (the asking of assistance) through the Prophets, the Messengers and the righteous scholars—is permissible after death, because the *muʿjiza* (staggering miracle) of the Prophets and the miraculous gifts of the Friends of Allah do not cease by virtue of their death. As for the Prophets - upon them peace - then that is because they are alive in their graves, praying and making the Hajj as transmitted in the reports, whereby their providing of assistance is a staggering miracle for them. And as for the Friends of Allah, then it is a miraculous gift for them." Nābulusī continued, "Our teacher [Khayr al-Dīn] al-Ramlī–Allah have mercy on him–said, 'The miraculous gifts are well-witnessed. It is not possible to deny them.' [He went on] until he said, 'As for kissing the tombs of the friends of Allah and their thresholds, there is no disagreement as to its permissibility. More than that, there is no dislike in kissing their thresholds for the sake of blessing.'"

For more on this subject see the documentation in *Tuḥfat al-labīb fī nuṣrat al-ḥabīb fīl-masāʾil al-ṣūfiyya* (The gift to the intelligent on the defense of the beloved regarding the Sufi questions) (Damascus 2007) on the permissibility of the above, especially according to Imam Aḥmad b. Ḥanbal and his school.

The dead hear the living, recognize them and return their salam

In *Tanwīr al-qulūb fī muʿāmalat ʿAllām al-ghuyūb* (Illumination of the hearts in interacting with the All-Knower of all unseens) by Shaykh Muḥammad Amīn b. Fatḥ Allāh Zādah al-Kurdī al-Irbilī al-Shāfiʿī al-Naqshbandī (d. 1322/1904) – Allah have mercy on him – the latter said, in the section entitled, *Faḍl al-awliyā' wa-thubūt karāmāti-him min al-Kitābi wal-Sunna* (The immense merit of the Friends of Allah and the established veracity of their miraculous gifts from the Book and the Sunna): "Know that all of the dwellers of the graves are alive with a *barzakhī* (interlife) kind of life by which they are cognizant, sentient, hearing and seeing; that they recognize whoever visits them and greets them and they return their salam; that they visit one another and they can feel hurt by what reaches them [of the news] of the living; that **they act with discretionary power, and there issues from them great matters** by the power of Allah – exalted is He; that they experience bliss or punishment; that the deeds of the living are shown to them, whereby whatever good they see give praise to Allah Most High, are elated by its good news and supplicate for the doer to have increase and remain firm upon it, and if they see evil they supplicate Allah on their behalf and say, 'O Allah, bring them back to obedience and guide them just as You guided us!'; and that they are aware of their states besides the deeds. For death is a move from one abode to another abode, and everything we have mentioned is firmly-established by the explicit text of the Sunna and the consensus of the Umma.

"As for the affirmation of the living of the dead, it was discussed already. As for their hearing, al-Bukhārī has narrated [also Muslim, both from Anas] that the Prophet–upon him the blessings and peace of Allah–said, 'When the deceased has been buried and his companions have walked away from him, he can hear the clatter of the shoes of his funeral party as they are leaving him.' Also in the two *Ṣaḥīḥ*s, another Prophetic report from Anas b. Mālik states – and this is Muslim's wording – that the Messenger of Allah–upon him the blessings and peace of Allah–left alone the bodies of those [of the unbelievers] that had been killed at Badr for three days, after which he came to them and stood over them, then he called them, saying, '**O Abū Jahl b. Hishām! O Umayya b. Khalaf! O ʿUtba b. Rabīʿa! O Shayba b. Rabīʿa! Is it not a fact that you have now certainly found what your nurturing Lord had promised to be true? For verily I have now certainly found what my nurturing Lord had promised me to be true!**'

يَا أَبَا جَهْلِ بْنَ هِشَامٍ يَا أُمَيَّةَ بْنَ خَلَفٍ يَا عُتْبَةَ بْنَ رَبِيعَةَ يَا شَيْبَةَ بْنَ رَبِيعَةَ
أَلَيْسَ قَدْ وَجَدْتُمْ مَا وَعَدَ رَبُّكُمْ حَقًّا؟
فَإِنِّي قَدْ وَجَدْتُ مَا وَعَدَنِي رَبِّي حَقًّا!

Whereupon 'Umar heard the statement of the Prophet, so he said, 'Messenger of Allah, how can they hear and from where can they answer, now that they have surely become corpses?' He replied, '**I swear by the One in Whose hand is my soul! All of you are not hearing what I say any better than they are. The only difference is that they are incapable of answering.**' Then he gave the order for them, so they were dragged off then they were thrown down the *qalīb* (unbuilt well) of Badr."

وَالَّذِى نَفْسِى بِيَدِهِ مَا أَنْتُمْ بِأَسْمَعَ لِمَا أَقُولُ مِنْهُمْ وَلَكِنَّهُمْ لاَ يَقْدِرُونَ أَنْ يُجِيبُوا. ثُمَّ أَمَرَ بِهِمْ فَسُحِبُوا فَأُلْقُوا فِى قَلِيبِ بَدْرٍ

He [=Shaykh Muḥammad Amīn al-Kurdī] said, "Any claim that it [=the hearing of the dead] was exclusive to that event necessitates evidence, which they will never find." He is alluding to whoever took the minority position that the dead do not hear. On this issue one can look up Ṭabarī's long rebuttal, in *Tahdhīb al-āthār* (5:485-521,

Musnad ʿUmar) of whoever made that claim, and his extensive review of the evidence showing that the dead hear the living. Allah grants success.

He continued, "As for the recognition of the dead for the visit of the living to them and their feeling elated about it, it is related from ʿĀʾisha – Allah be well-pleased with her – that she said, 'The Messenger of Allah –upon him the blessings and peace of Allah– said, "**No man visits his brother's grave and sits besides it but the latter welcomes his company and responds to him until he gets up**."'

مَا مِنْ رَجُلٍ يَزُورُ قَبْرَ أَخِيهِ وَيَجْلِسُ عِنْدَهُ
إِلَّا اسْتَأْنَسَ بِهِ وَرَدَّ عَلَيْهِ حَتَّى يَقُومَ

The Hadith master al-ʿIrāqī said in the documentation of the *Iḥyāʾ*, 'Ibn Abī al-Dūnyā documented it in *al-Qubūr* and therein is ʿAbd Allāh b. Simʿān, whose state I have not yet ascertained, and Ibn ʿAbd al-Barr narrated something like it in *al-Tamhīd* from Ibn ʿAbbās, which ʿAbd al-Ḥaqq al-Ishbīlī rated sound.' The Hadith master Ibn Ḥajar said in *Lisān al-Mīzān*, 'It is possible that he [=ʿAbd Allāh b. Simʿān] is the one that was cited in some of the books, namely ʿAbd Allāh b. Ziyād b. Simʿān – he is frequently identified by his grandfather – and he is of the weak narrators, but the Hadith master Murtaḍā al-Zabīdī said in the *Itḥāf*, 'If he happens to be ʿAbd Allāh b. Muḥammad b. Abī Yaḥyā then he is trustworthy and this is apparently the case, for he is identified by his grandfather.'"

Then al-Kurdī mentioned Abū Hurayra's hadith – Allah be well-pleased with him, "When a man passes by a grave that he recognizes and he gives salam to him [=the one buried there], the latter returns his salam and recognizes him, and if he passes by a grave he does not recognize and gives salam to him, the latter returns his salam."

إِذَا مَرَّ الرَّجُلُ بِقَبْرٍ يَعْرِفُهُ فَسَلَّمَ عَلَيْهِ رَدَّ عَلَيْهِ السَّلَامَ وَعَرَفَهُ، وَإِذَا مَرَّ بِقَبْرٍ لَا يَعْرِفُهُ فَسَلَّمَ عَلَيْهِ رَدَّ عَلَيْهِ السَّلَامَ

Ibn Abī al-Dunyā narrated it and, through the latter, al-Bayhaqī in the *Shuʿāb* and al-Ṣābūnī in *al-Miʾatayn*, all as Abū Hurayra's own statement. It is supported by the report from al-Rabīʿ b. Sulaymān al-Muʾadhdhin who said Bishr b. Bakr narrated to them, from al-Awzāʿī, from ʿAṭāʾ, from Ibn ʿAbbās, that the Messenger of Allah –upon him the blessings and peace of Allah– said, "**None passes by the grave of his brother believer whom he knew in life and greets him but the latter recognizes him and returns his salam.**"

مَا مِنْ أَحَدٍ يَمُرُّ عَلَى قَبْرِ أَخِيهِ الْمُؤْمِنِ كَانَ يَعْرِفُهُ فِي الدُّنْيَا يُسَلِّمُ عَلَيْهِ إِلَّا عَرَفَهُ وَرَدَّ عَلَيْهِ السَّلَامَ

Ibn ʿAbd al-Barr documented it and ʿAbd al-Ḥaqq said its chain is sound.

Then he mentioned the Prophetic hadith from Abū Hurayra, "**Make beautiful the shrouds of your deceased ones, for verily they visit one another in their graves.**"

حَسِّنُوا أَكْفَانَ مَوْتَاكُمْ فَإِنَّهُمْ يَتَزَاوَرُونَ فِي قُبُورِهِمْ

Ibn ʿAdī narrated it in *al-Kāmil* (Complete compendium of weak narrators) and it is cited in the books of forgeries but al-Suyūṭī said in the *Laʾāliʾ*, "The hadith is fair and sound, it has many paths of transmission and witness reports which I collected in *Sharḥ al-ṣudūr*." Then al-Kurdī said, "As for the dead getting hurt by what the living do then the Prophet –upon him the blessings and peace of Allah– said, '**Verily the deceased is hurt in his grave by whatever would hurt him in his own house.**'"

إِنَّ الْمَـيِّتَ يُؤْذِيهِ فِي قَبْرِهِ مَا يُؤْذِيهِ فِي بَيْتِهِ

Kalābādhī narrated it in *Baḥr al-fawā'id* and *Miftāḥ al-ma'ānī* through Ibn Lahī'a, from 'Ā'isha. Abū Ḥātim rated it "disclaimed" in his *'Ilal* but Sakhāwī said in the *Maqāṣid*, "Witnessing to it is what Abū Dāwūd, Ibn Mājah and others narrated [from her], from the Prophet –upon him the blessings and peace of Allah– '**Breaking the bone of the dead is like breaking his bone when he was alive.**'"

كَسْرُ عَظْمِ المَيِّتِ كَكَسْرِ عَظْمِهِ حَيّاً

Discussion on the discretionary power of *Awliyā* in their graves

Al-Kurdī went on, "As for the *taṣarruf* (discretionary power) of the dead and the issuing of orders from them by the power of Allah Most High, then it was narrated that the Messenger of Allah –upon him the blessings and peace of Allah–after the killing of Ja'far [b. Abī Ṭālib at the battle of Mu'ta] said, '**I recognized Ja'far among some angel companions of his giving the glad tidings of rain to the people of Bīsha.**' The latter is a region in Yemen."

عَرَفْتُ جَعْفَراً فِي رُفْقَةٍ مِنَ المَلاَئِكَةِ يُبَشِّرُونَ أَهْلَ بِيشَةَ بِالمَطَرِ.

وبِيشة بكسر أوله بلدة في اليمن

Ibn 'Adī and Ibn 'Asākir narrated it from 'Alī b. Abī Ṭālib – Allah be well-pleased with him – and it is a weak narration per al-Suyūṭī but it has a number of witness-reports. He continued: "As for the bliss of the dead and their punishment, such has been related from the Prophet –

upon him blessings and peace– through mass transmission meaning-wise, and the people of the Sunna and the Congregation certainly concur that the bliss of the grave and its punishment are true and that it is obligatory to believe in them, and that bliss and punishment take effect on both the spirit and the body, because the doing of sins and acts of obedience is with both of them.

"As for the bliss of the Prophets–upon them peace–in their graves, we have already mentioned that they are alive in their graves, tender, praying. It has also been transmitted in the sound hadiths that they perform Hajj, and Allah may honor with that some of the people of the interlife even if they have no obtained any reward for it since death put an end to their deeds, but Allah lets their performance of deeds endure for them so that they will delight in the remembrance of Allah and in obedience to Him in the same way the angels and the people of goodness in Paradise delight in that, because **remembrance of Allah and obedience are inherently greater for their doers than all of the bliss of the people of the world and its pleasures**. As for the hadith, '**When a human being dies, his deeds have ceased but for three things**' [*Ṣaḥīḥ Muslim*]

إِذَا مَاتَ الإِنْسَانُ انْقَطَعَ عَمَلُهُ إِلاَّ مِنْ ثَلاثٍ

which the Prophet–upon him the blessings and peace of Allah–excepted, its meaning is the ceasing of the reward of deeds, not of the deeds themselves, so that it is reconciled with the rest of the evidence, as is obvious for anyone proficient in the Sunna who is free of proclivity to whims–Allah protect us from them with His bounty.

"As for the punishment of the grave for some of the dead, then Allah Most High has related about the House of Fir'awn that *the Fire—they are exposed to it early in the day and late* (Ghāfir 40:46),

﴿ ٱلنَّارُ يُعْرَضُونَ عَلَيْهَا غُدُوًّا وَعَشِيًّا ﴾

and the Prophet –upon him the blessings and peace of Allah– said, '**Were it not that you would end up not burying one another I would have supplicated Allah to let you hear the punishment of the grave that He has let me hear**.'" Aḥmad, al-Ḥākim and al-Ṭabarī in *Tahdhīb al-āthār* narrated it from Anas and its basis is in *Ṣaḥīḥ Muslim* without "that He has let me hear."

لَوْلاَ أَنْ لاَ تَدَافَنُوا لَدَعَوْتُ الله أَنْ يُسْمِعَكُمْ عَذَابَ الْقَبْرِ مَا أَسْمَعَنِي

Al-Kurdī went on: "As for the exposure of the deeds of the living to the dead then he –upon him the blessings and peace of Allah– has said, '**Your deeds are displayed to the dead, so if they see goodness they are happy and elated at the glad tidings, and if they see evil they say, "O Allah! Give him another chance."'**

تُعْرَضُ أَعْمَالُكُمْ عَلَى الْمَوْتَى، فَإِنْ رَأَوْا حَسَناً فَرِحُوا وَاسْتَبْشَرُوا، وَإِنْ رَأَوا سُوأً قَالُوا: اللهمَّ رَاجِعْ بِهِ

Ibn al-Mubārak narrated it." The latter is actually a statement of Abū Ayyūb al-Anṣārī narrated by Ibn Abī al-Dunyā in *al-Manāmāt*, but Suyūṭī has mentioned in *Sharḥ al-ṣudūr* no less than 15 proofs in the chapter on the exposure of the deeds of the living to the dead. Among the best of them is the Prophetic report from Anas by Aḥmad, Ṭabarānī in *al-Kabīr* and al-Ḥakīm al-Tirmidhī, "**Verily your deeds are shown to your close relatives and your kindred among the dead, so if there is goodness they become elated at the glad tidings, and if it is otherwise they say, 'O Allah! Do not cause them to die before You guide them just as You guided us!'**"

إنّ أعْمالَكُمْ تُعْرَضُ على أقارِبِكُمْ وعَشَائِرِكُمْ مِنَ الأمْوَاتِ فإنْ كانَ خَيْراً اسْتَبْشَرُوا وإنْ كانَ غَيْرَ ذلِكَ قالوا اللهمَّ لا تُمِتْهُمْ حَتَّى تَهْدِيَهُمْ كما هَدَيْتَنا

Ṭayālisī also narrated the same in his *Musnad* from Jābir and something similar from Abū Hurayra. Also narrated as Prophetic reports from (i) al-Nuʿmān b. Bashīr by al-Bukhārī in his *Tārīkh*, al-Ḥākim, Bayhaqī in the *Shuʿab*, al-Dūlābī in *al-Kunā wal-asmā'*, Ibn Abī al-Dunyā in *al-Manāmāt* and Ibn ʿAsākir in *Tārīkh Dimashq*: "**[Beware] Allah! [Beware] Allah with respect to your brethren in the graves! For your deeds are shown to them;**"

اللهَ اللهَ فِي إِخْوَانِكُمْ مِنْ أَهْلِ الْقُبُورِ، فَإِنَّ أَعْمَالَكُمْ تُعْرَضُ عَلَيْهِمْ

and (ii) Abū Hurayra by Ibn Abī al-Dunyā and others: "**Do not shame your deceased ones with the bad deeds that you do, for they are exposed to your kindred of the people of the graves.**"

لَا تَفْضَحُوا مَوْتَاكُمْ بِسَيِّئَاتِ أَعْمَالِكُمْ، فَإِنَّهَا تُعْرَضُ عَلَى أَوْلِيَائِكُمْ مِنْ أَهْلِ الْقُبُورِ

Hence Abū al-Dardā' would seek refuge in Allah from doing any deed that might hurt his maternal uncle ʿAbd Allāh b. Rawāḥa, as narrated by Ibn al-Mubārak, Ibn Abī al-Dunyā and others.

Lastly al-Kurdī said, "As for their knowledge if the states of the people living in the world other than the latter's deeds and their seeing them, the Prophet –upon him blessings and peace of Allah– said, '**Verily the deceased one recognizes whoever carries him, whoever washes him and whoever lets him down into his grave.**'"

إِنَّ الْمَيِّتَ يَعْرِفُ مَنْ يَحْمِلُهُ وَمَنْ يُغَسِّلُهُ وَمَنْ يُدَلِّيهِ فِي قَبْرِهِ

It is narrated from Abū Sa'īd al-Khudrī by Aḥmad, al-Ṭabarānī in *al-Awsaṭ*, al-Khaṭīb in *al-Tārīkh* and Abū Nu'aym in *Akhbār Aṣbahān.*

Also among the useful references on the subject: *Karāmāt al-awliyā* by al-La'la'ākī, *Juz' karāmāt al-awliyā'* by al-Khallāl, Ibn 'Abd al-Salām's fatwa in *al-Fatāwā al-mawṣiliyya*, al-Nawawī's explanation on Anas's report in *Sharḥ Ṣaḥīḥ Muslim*, Ibn al-Qayyim in the opening chapter of *Kitāb al-Rūḥ*, Ibn Ḥajar's *al-Jawāb al-kāfī 'an al-su'āl al-khāfī*, al-Sakhāwī in *al-Īḍāḥ wal-tabyīn fī mas'alat al-talqīn*, al-Suyūṭī in the opening fatwa of the first part of the responses on Resurrection in *al-Ḥāwī lil-Fatāwā*, Ibn Mughayzīl in *al-Kawākib al-zāhira fī ijtimā' al-awliyā' yaqaẓatan bi-Sayyid al-dunyā wal-ākhira*, 'Abd al-Bāqī al-Khazrajī in *al-Suyūf al-ṣiqāl fī raqabat man ankara karāmāt al-awliyā' ba'da al-intiqāl*, and others.

VI
Fatwas of the jurists on the status of vows on behalf of a *walī* and sacrifices performed over a *walī*'s grave

The knower of Allah and jurist ʿAbd al-Ghanī al-Nābulusī al-Dimashqī al-Ṣāliḥī – Allah sanctify his secret – also said in *Sharḥ al-ṭarīqat al-Muḥammadiyya*, as related by ʿAlāʾ al-Dīn Ibn ʿĀbidīn in *al-Hadiyyat al-ʿAlāʾiyya*, a compendium on Ḥanafī fiqh: "Deriving blessing from the burial places of the Friends of Allah and the righteous and making vows on their behalf when asking for some cure or for the return of someone missing is only another name for giving alms to the maintainers of their graves, as the jurists have said concerning whoever remits a poor person zakat and names it a loan: it is correct, because what matters is the meaning and not the wording. Likewise alms given to a wealthy person is a gift, whereas the gift given to a poor person is alms. Ibn Ḥajar al-Haytamī al-Shāfiʿī has explicitly states in his fatwas, 'This vow that is made for the deceased *walī*, when the vower intends thereby another act of drawing near [to Allah], such as [supporting] the children of the deceased *walī*, or his successors, or feeding the poor that are at his grave the vow is sound and it is obligatory to spend it on what the vower intended, etc.' Most people in our time intend that, so the discourse is understood in this sense and the preacher ought not to forbid what one of the imams of the Muslims has said.

"Rather any prohibition should bear on what has been agreed upon as prohibited by consensus of the imams and which is part of what is necessarily known in the faith, such as the prohibitiveness of fornication, consuming usury, drinking intoxicants, thinking ill of Muslims, usurping possessions, bribery, arrogance, vainglory, dishonoring the Muslims and spreading indecency among them, attacking the Friends of Allah in ignorance of the meaning of their discourse and inability to see the utter harmony of their speech with the speech of Allah Most High and His Messenger, denying their miraculous gifts, forbidding people from deriving blessing from them, and other than that of the ugly behavior that most of the people of our countries practice nowadays. We ask Allah for safety!"

Of the reliable sources on this subject are the following:

I. Shaykh Sulaymān b. ʿAbd al-Wahhāb al-Najdī's published refutation of the claim by his brother Muḥammad b. ʿAbd al-Wahhāb (the founder of the Wahhābī sect) in the latter's book *al-Uṣūl al-thalātha* (The three principles) that the person making a vow and the person slaughtering a sacrifice on the grave of a *walī* are unbelievers, entitled *al-Radd ʿalā man kaffara al-muslimīna bi-sababi al-nadhri li-ghayri-l-Lāh* (Refutation of him who declared the Muslims unbelievers because of vows for other than Allah). It is ms. 6805 at the Awqāf Baghdād library according to Khayr al-Dīn al-Ziriklī;

II. another refutation of Wahhabism by the same author entitled *al-Ṣawāʿiq al-ilāhiyya ʿalā madhhab al-wahhābiyya* (The divine thunderbolts against the school of the Wahhabis) from which our teachers' teacher Shaykh al-ʿArabī al-Tabbānī (Abū Marzūq) quoted extensively in his book *Barāʾat al-Ashʿariyyīn* (The innocence of the Ashʿarīs, 1:150-159) and which has been published in full;

III. the fatwa of the Mufti of the Shāfiʿīs in Medina, the transmissologist Muḥammad b. Sulaymān al-Kurdī (1125-1194/1713-1780) which the jurist al-Ḥabīb ʿAlawī b. Aḥmad b. Ḥasan al-Ḥaddād (1163-1232/1750-1817) quoted in his book *Miṣbāh al-anām fī raddi shubuhāt al-Najdī al-bidʿī al-latī aḍalla bihā al-ʿawāmm* (The light of mankind: refutation of the fallacies of the innovator from Najd by which he has led the general population astray), first published in 1216/1801 and again in 1325/1907 at al-Maṭbaʿat al-Sharafiyya in Cairo (in 17 chapters he epitomized in his introduction, which we have translated in full);[1]

[1] archive.org/details/Misbah-al-Anam-Habib-Alawi-ibn-Ahmad-al-Haddad

IV. the answer penned by the Indian *muḥaddith* Shams al-Ḥaqq al-ʿAẓīm Ābādī al-Ṣiddīqī (1857-1911) in the first article of his epistle *Ghunyat al-almaʿī* (Sufficiency of the wise), in the beginning of which he states, "sacrifices performed on behalf of the dead are a Sunna and their reward reaches them without the shadow of a doubt." This epistle was published at the end of one of the editions of al-Ṭabarānī's *al-Muʿjam al-ṣaghīr.*

V. The very beneficial answer given by our Shaykh the jurist al-Ḥabīb Zayn al-ʿĀbidīn b. Ibrāhīm b. Zayn b. Sumayṭ al-Shāfiʿī al-Madanī in the 2000 edition of his book *al-Ajwibat al-ghāliya fī ʿaqīdat al-firqat al-nājiya* (The precious answers regarding the doctrinal creed of the saved group) pp. 125-128.

Additional stirring hadiths and reports on the interlife

The following text is from the book entitled *Aḥkām tamannī al-mawt* which is established as a compilation by Muḥammad b. ʿAbd al-Wahhāb al-Najdī per its al-Maktabat al-Saʿūdiyya ms. 86/771 in Riyadh. It is all excerpts from reliable books without comment.

"[It is narrated] in al-Bayhaqī [in *Dalāʾil al-nubuwwa*] from Anas: "Umar equipped an army an put al-ʿAlāʾ b. al-Ḥaḍramī in command of it. I was among its raiders. As we returned he died on the way so we buried him. A man came after we had finished his burial and asked, "Who is this?" We said, "This is the best of people. This is Ibn al-Ḥaḍramī." He said, "Verily this land spits out the dead. Why do you not transfer him somewhere a mile or or two miles off, where the land accepts the dead?" So we started digging him out but when we reached the grave side-niche, behold! Our friend was no longer there, and behold! The side-niche had stretched in the form of a shining light as far as the eye could see. So we threw back the soil, after which we departed.' Ibn al-Jawzī mentioned from Jaʿfar al-Sarrāj, from one of his shaykhs: 'A certain grave was uncovered in the vicinity of Imam Aḥmad, and behold! On top of the deceased's chest there was a fragrant plant quivering.'

"Ibn Abī al-Dunyā [narrated] from Miskīn b. Bukayr [or 'Sukayn b. Mukayn, a man from the Banū 'Ijl' per the printed edition of Ibn Abī al-Dunyā's *al-Riqqa wal-bukā'* (Soft-heartedness and weeping)] that when Warrād al-'Ijlī died and they carried him to his burial place, they went down first to help lower him down into it, and – behold! – the whole grave was carpeted with fragrant plants. One of those that went down into the pit took some of it home. It remained tender and unchanged for seventy days. People would come to see it morning and evening. The crowds grew around that, to the point the emir feared that people would fall into some strife, so he sent [some officer] to the man who took that fragrant plant from him and dispersed the crowds. Later the emir could no longer find it wher it had been put and never found out how it had disappeared.

"Al-Khaṭib [narrated] from Muḥammad b. Mukhallad al-'Aṭṭār who said, 'When my mother died and I was burying her in the Dharb al-rayḥān cemetery, I went down to dispose her into her side-niche myself when some hole opened up exposing the grave adjacent to it. Behold! There was a man in a new shroud and on top of his chest there was a bunch of fresh jasmin. I took it and smelled it. It was more fragrant than musk. A group of people that were with me in the funeral also smelled it. Then I returned it to its spot and walled up the hole.' [It is also narrated] in Ibn Sa'd's *Ṭabaqāt* from Abū Sa'īd al-Khudrī that he said, 'I was among those that dug a grave for Sa'd b. Mu'ādh in al-Baqī', and musk kept exuding in our faces the more we dug.' He also narrated from Muḥammad b. Shuraḥbīl b. Ḥasana that he said, 'Someone took a handful of the earth of Sa'd's grave home with him. Later, when he looked at it, behold! It was musk.'

"Bayhaqī [in *Shuʿab al-īmān*] narrated with a fair chain [per al-Mundhirī in *al-Targhīb* and al-Suyūṭī in *Sharḥ al-ṣudūr*] from Ibn ʿUmar, that a desert Arab died as a shahid while fighting by the Prophet's side. The latter–upon him the blessings and peace of Allah–sat by him cheerful and smiling, then he turned away from him. Asked about it he said, **'As for my cheerfulness it was for what I saw of the honorable status of his soul for Allah; and as for my turning away from him it is because his wife of the beautiful-eyed women of Paradise is now at his bedside.'**

أَمَّا مَا رَأَيْتُمْ مِنِ اسْتِبْشَارِي - أَوْ قَالَ: سُرُورِي - فَلِمَا رَأَيْتُ مِنْ كَرَامَةِ رُوحِهِ عَلَى اللهِ تَعَالَى، وَأَمَّا إِعْرَاضِي عَنْهُ، فَإِنَّ زَوْجَتَهُ مِنَ الْحُورِ الْعِينِ الْآنَ عِنْدَ رَأْسِهِ

Aḥmad and al-Ḥākim also narrate from ʿĀʾisha–Allah be well-pleased with her–that she said, 'I would enter the house and undress, saying: "This is only my father and my husband." But when ʿUmar was buried with them I no longer entered it other than fully dressed, out of modesty before ʿUmar.' Bayhaqī and Ḥākim also narrated from Abū Hurayra the Prophetic hadith, **'I bear witness that these are shahids in the presence of Allah on the Day of Resurrection, so come to them and visit them. By the One in Whose hand is my soul none of you greets them to the Day of Resurrection but they definitely answer him,'** i.e. Muṣʿab b. ʿUmayr and his companions. [Its chain is fair.]

أَشْهَدُ أَنَّ هٰؤُلَاءِ شُهَدَاءُ عِنْدَ اللهِ إِلَى يَوْمِ الْقِيَامَةِ فَأْتُوهُمْ وَزُورُوهُمْ. وَالَّذِي نَفْسِي بِيَدِهِ لَا يُسَلِّمُ عَلَيْهِمْ أَحَدٌ إِلَى يَوْمِ الْقِيَامَةِ إِلَّا رَدُّوا عَلَيْهِ

Al-Ṭabarānī also brought it out in *al-Muʿjam al-Kabīr* and *al-Awsaṭ*, as did Abū Nuʿaym in *al-Ḥilya*. Al-Ḥākim also narrated—

declaring it *ṣaḥīḥ*—from ʿAbd Allāh b. Abī Farwa that **the Prophet**–upon him the blessings and peace of Allah–**visited the graves of the shahids at Uḥud then he said, 'O Allah, our nurturing Lord! Verily your servant and Prophet bears witness that these ones are shahids and that whoever visits them and greets them, until the Day of Resurrection, they definitely answer him.'** [Al-Bayhaqī also narrated it in the *Dalāʾil* in mursal mode.]

اللَّهُمَّ إِنَّ عَبْدَكَ وَنَبِيَّكَ يَشْهَدُ أَنَّ هٰؤُلَاءِ شُهَدَاءُ وَأَنَّهُ مَنْ زَارَهُمْ وَسَلَّمَ عَلَيْهِمْ إِلَى يَوْمِ الْقِيَامَةِ رَدُّوا عَلَيْهِ

"Ibn Saʿd also narrated from Ibn al-Musayyib that the latter used to keep to the Mosque on the Days of al-Ḥarra while people were killing one another and that he said, 'Whenever it was time for the prayer I would hear an *adhān* coming out of the Prophetic grave.' Al-Khaṭīb also narrated from Ibrāhīm b. Ismāʿīl b. Khalaf that he said, 'Aḥmad b. Naṣr [b. Mālik al-Khuzāʿī (d. 231/846)] was my close friend. When he was killed [by the Abbasid Caliph al-Wāthiq bi-l-Lāh] during the [Muʿtazilī] ordeal and he was crucified [in Sāmarrāʾ], I was told that his [decapitated] head [on a stake in Baghdad] would recite the Qurʾān. So I went [to see], and I spent the night near the head, overlooking it. There were footmen and riders guarding it. When the fountains were shut down I heard the head reciting, *Alif lām mīm. Have people reckoned that they would be left alone for saying, "We believe," while they will not be tested?* (al-ʿAnkabūt 29:1-2).

﴿ الٓمٓ ١ أَحَسِبَ ٱلنَّاسُ أَن يُتۡرَكُوٓاْ أَن يَقُولُوٓاْ ءَامَنَّا وَهُمۡ لَا يُفۡتَنُونَ ٢ ﴾

العنكبوت

At this goose-bumps stood on my flesh. Then I saw him after that in my sleep, wearing silk and brocade and crowned with a diadem. I said, "What has Allah done with you O my brother?" He said, "He has forgiven me and He has made me enter Paradise, except that I was anxious for three days." "Why?" I said. He said, "I saw the Messenger of Allah–upon him blessings and peace of Allah–pass by me, but when he reached my wooden stake he turned his face away from me. I asked him after that, 'Messenger of Allah! Was I killed for the sake of the truth or for the sake of falsehood?' He said, 'You followed the truth, but the one that killed you is a man from the people of my House, so when I reached you I was ashamed before you.'""

"Ibn ʿAsākir also narrated through Abū Ṣāliḥ—al-Layth's scribe—from Yaḥyā b. Ayyūb al-Khuzāʿī that the latter said, 'I heard someone mention that there was, in the time of ʿUmar b. al-Khaṭṭāb, a young man who prayed assiduously and who kept to the Mosque. ʿUmar admired him. He had an aged father. After he finished praying he would always go to take care of his father. His itinerary passed by the door of a woman who became infatuated with him. She would make sure to stand in his way. One night he passed by her and she kept enticing him until he followed her. When she reached her door she entered and he was about to enter when he remembered Allah. His state was lifted from him and this verse appeared on his tongue, *verily those that beware when some imaginary suggestion from the devil touches them, they remember; then behold: they are wide awake* (Aʿrāf 7:201).

﴿ إِنَّ ٱلَّذِينَ ٱتَّقَوْاْ إِذَا مَسَّهُمْ طَـٰٓئِفٌ مِّنَ ٱلشَّيْطَـٰنِ تَذَكَّرُواْ فَإِذَا هُم
مُّبْصِرُونَ ﴿٢٠١﴾ ﴾ الأعراف

Thereupon the young man fell unconscious. The woman called for her maid and they both carried him to his door and left him there. His father was wondering where he was so he came out looking for him and saw him lying there unconscious. He called for one of his household. They carried him inside. He came to a long while later during the night. His father asked him, "My son, what happened to you?" He said, "Goodness." Then he told him the whole thing. His father said, "My son, and what verse did you recite?" He recited the same verse he had recited and again fell unconscious. They moved him and—behold!—he had died. They washed him, brought him out and buried him at night. In the morning the news was conveyed to 'Umar–Allah be well-pleased with him–who came to the father and condoled with him. He asked him, "You should have told me." He said, "Commander of the believers, it was night." 'Umar said, "So take us to his grave." When they reached it 'Umar said, "O So and so! *and for whoever fears the station of his nurturing Lord there are two gardens*—(al-Raḥmān 55:46).

﴿ وَلِمَنْ خَافَ مَقَامَ رَبِّهِۦ جَنَّتَانِ ﴿٤٦﴾ ﴾ الرحمن

The young man answered him from inside the grave, "O 'Umar! My nurturing Lord has certainly given them to me in Paradise twice.'"

"Al-Bayhaqī and others also narrated from Abū 'Uthmān al-Nahdī, from Mīnā or Ibn Mīnā or Mīnās or Sās, that the latter went out one warm day wearing light clothes to attend a funeral. He said, 'I ended up near some grave. I prayed two quick cycles in its vicinity then I laid down on top of the grave. I swear by Allah that I was indeed wide awake when I suddenly heard a voice in the grave saying. 'Get up! You are harming me!' Then the voice said, 'Verily you indeed perform deeds but you do not know, whereas we do know but we do not perform deeds. I swear by Allah that if I had prayed the like of those two quick cycles of yours, it would have been lovelier to me than the whole world and everything in it.' [Ibn Abī al-Dunyā cited it in *al-Qubūr* and al-Bayhaqī in the *Dalā'il* and the *Shu'ab.*] Al-Bukhārī in his *Tārīkh* and others also narrated from 'Abd Allāh b. 'Ubayd al-Anṣārī that he said, 'I was among those that buried Thābit b. Qays b. Shammās who had been struck on the Day of Yamāma (11/632). When we brought him into his grave we heard him say, "Muḥammad is the Messenger of Allah. Abū Bakr is the most truthful one. 'Umar is the shahid. 'Uthmān is gentle, merciful." We all took a look at him but behold, he was dead.'""

VII
Visiting the Friends of Allah for the good pleasure of Allah: etiquette, merits and intention of visitation

The Messenger of Allah–upon him blessings and peace– said,

نَهَيْتُكُمْ عَنْ زِيَارَةِ الْقُبُورِ فَزُورُوهَا

"I had forbidden you from visiting the graves. Now do visit them!" Muslim and others narrated it from Burayda. One narration has,

نَهَيْتُكُمْ عَنْ ثَلاَثٍ وَأَنَا آمُرُكُمْ بِهِنَّ، نَهَيْتُكُمْ عَنْ زِيَارَةِ الْقُبُورِ فَزُورُوهَا

"I had forbidden you three things and I myself am now commanding you to do them. I had forbidden you from visiting the graves, so do visit them now." Abū Dāwūd narrated it. Mālik and al-Shāfiʿī also narrated it from Abū Saʿīd al-Khudrī, and Ahmad from ʿAlī and Ibn Masʿūd. Ibn Abī al-Dunyā and al-Bayhaqī in the *Shuʿab* narrated from Muḥammad b. Wāsiʿ that he said, "It has reached me that the dead know well of their visitors on the day of Jumuʿa and one day before it and one day after it." Suyūṭī mentioned it in *Sharḥ al-ṣudūr*. This includes all Muslims, so the status of the Friends of Allah is higher, and the status of the Prophets is higher than the latter.

Al-Rawwās–Allah sanctify his secret–said in *Bawāriq al-ḥaqāʾiq* (The lightning flashes of spiritual realities) that Zayn al-ʿĀbidīn–Allah be well-pleased with him–said, "Whoever leaves his house to visit someone who is a Friend of Allah Most High does not cease to probe deep into mercy until he returns to his original place. And the sins of a thousand years are forgiven for him, And he shall be tomorrow in the vicinity of the All-Beneficent." His son al-Bāqir said–Allah be well-pleased with him–"If the visitor knew who he was visiting and what he has of reward, he would walk even on the apple of his eyes and not just his feet." The Knower of Allah al-Bajalī, i.e. Nūr al-Dīn Muḥammad b. Jarīr b. al-Ḥasan b. 'Alī al-Yamānī, a descendant of the Companion Jarīr b. 'Abd Allāh al-Bajalī–may Allah be well-pleased with him–saw the Messenger of Allah–upon him the blessings and peace of Allah–in dream and he said, "O Messenger of Allah, teach me something." He said to him–upon him the blessings and peace of Allah–"Your standing before someone who is a Friend of Allah if only for the time it takes to milk a ewe or grill an egg is better for you than to worship Allah until you are cut down limb by limb." Al-Bajalī said, "Living or dead?" He answered, "Whether he is 'living' or 'dead'." Al-Shirwānī said in his glosses on Ibn Ḥajar al-Haytamī's *Tuḥfat al-muḥtāj*, a commentary on al-Nawawī's *al-Minhāj* in Shāfi'ī fiqh: "The visit to the graves is highly recommended for the purpose of contemplation, or the invocation of mercy, or recitation and supplication **or deriving blessing, which is a Sunna with respect to the people of goodness for they have in their *barāzikh* (interlives) *taṣarrufāt* (discretionary powers) and blessings whose number is beyond count.**" All of the above was mentioned by al-Rawwās in *Bawāriq al-ḥaqā'iq*.

The Mālikī Master 'Abd al-Ḥaqq al-Ishbīlī set apart a chapter in his book *al-'Āqiba* (The hereafter) entitled "Mention of the dreams seen about some of the righteous ones showing what they bask in of goddness and an excellent aftermath." For **the truthful vision is one of the gates of Prophetic knowledge as related from Imam Mālik** by Ibn 'Abd al-Barr in *al-Tamhīd* and Qadi 'Iyāḍ in the chapter on dream interpretation in his commentary on *Ṣaḥīḥ Muslim*.

The author of *Tanbīh al-sālikīn ilā ghurūr al-mutashayyikhīn* (Notification to the wayfarers about the delusion of would-be shaykhs) said: "As for the etiquettes of the visitation to the Prophets and *Awliyā*, let the murid use as an intermediary the *rūḥāniyya* (spiritual presence) of his *murshid* who has immersed him in his goodness, and let his take him as his interceding advocate to the court of that one who is being visited at the beginning of his progress. Let him notice him before himself in the style of intercessors on behalf of a disobedient people, and let him ask forgiveness abundantly for all his sins and for breaking his promise; nay, for his very 'knowledge' and 'merit' and 'asceticism'! And let him regard himself as bankrupt of righteous work. And he does not feel hurt by the arduousness of the way but rather count it as a bounty and a blessing from Allah Most High. For there is in that an indication of the obtainment of the goal, just as befell Mūsā with al-Khaḍir–upon both of them peace–in the statement of Allah Most High, *'We have no doubt met with fatigue in this journey of ours'* (al-Kahf 18:62).

﴿لَقَدْ لَقِينَا مِن سَفَرِنَا هَٰذَا نَصَبًا﴾ الكهف ٦٢

"And he makes pure, in the presence of the grave, the outward and the inward intention, and he greets him from all of its doors with lowliness and broken-heartedness upon approaching due to his dear hope, and he sayd, '*as-salāmu 'alaykum*, a greeting from me to you,' and he recites at every door al-Fātiḥa and al-Ikhlāṣ three times each, and he said, 'I see you as my intermediary to the nurturing Lord of humankind for the facilitation of my affairs in this life and the next.'

"And it is best for him not to intend by that visitation other than the good pleasure of the pure divine Essence, not some lowly matter. Then, **when his sight falls upon the cradle of the presence of the grave, he recites the Fatiha in every step forward he takes up to seven steps, and he ties up his heart with the heart of the presence of the grave per the *wuqūf qalbī*** (heart's undivided attention) **for the outpouring from his inwardness—it is the same whether he is of 'the living' or of 'the dead'—then he stands, fully orienting himself to the grave of the one he is visiting, near where the latter's feet are with his back to the qibla, noticing his own *murshid* as his intercessor in the presence of the one being visited, and using that intercessor as his intermediary to him**. At that time he greets him and recites the Fatīḥa and al-Ikhlāṣ, standing as if he were alive and he were standing right before him. Then if he sits and recites one tenth of the Qur'ān it is better. Then he receives the outpourings of his heart, making his heart adhere to the heart of the one he is visiting but ensuring that his own heart is in a lower position. And let him not be inadvertent of the *wuqūf qalbī* with utmost humble supplication and broken-heartedness; and let him have no distraction; and let him keep the best opinion if he has a particular need, for it will be fulfilled by his intermediary with the permission of my nurturing Lord. Allah Most High said, '**I am according to My servant's thought about Me**.' It is agreed upon.

قال الله تعالى: **أَنَا عِنْدَ ظَنِّ عَبْدِي بِي**. متفق عليه

"**The duration of that *istifāḍa*** (spiritual outpouring) **depends on one's sojourn and is according to one's spiritual taste and *jamʿiyya*** (spiritual self-collectedness) **and manners**. Then he supplicates for himself and for the believing men and the believing women by saying, 'O Allah, forgive me and the believing men and the believing women, the living and the dead,' and **he focuses especially on himself and his *murshid* with righteous supplications, and he uses as his intermediary the one being visited – by means of the *rābiṭa* (heart-fastening) to his *murshid* who is supplicating for him to Allah so that He will make him obtain of His goodness and His bestowal. He must be certain that his supplications will be answered**. For never does he supplicate for anything permissible but the one in the place of repose says *āmīn* to his prayer, whereupon Allah shall answer him out of His bounty and special care. When he wants to depart and he is standing up, he gives salam as he did the first time and recites the Fātiḥa and al-Ikhlāṣ, or with a tenth of the Qur'ān, and he takes him as his intermediary to his nurturing Lord in all his worldly and next-worldly affairs, and he does that at each of his doors, and he leaves backside first. Once he has done that, his quest has been obtained, and he has received help to victory, and every evil and harm has been severed from him." Thus in *Tanbīh al-sālikīn* by the Shaykh Ḥasan b. Muḥammad

Ḥilmī al-Quḥḥī al-Dāghistānī (p. 422 of the Dār al-Nuʿmān ed.), "from the *Mutammimāt*, p. 206" i.e. the completions of by Shaykh Ḍiyāʾ al-Dīn al-Kumushkhānawī's *Jāmiʿ uṣūl al-awliyāʾ* (Compendium of the foundational principles of the Friends of Allah) whose main part we read with Shaykh Muḥammad Saʿīd al-Kaḥīl al-Ḥimṣī al-Shādhilī al-Naqshbandī–Allah have mercy on them.

VIII
Mawlana Khālid on being with one's *murshid* at all times

Al-Quḥḥī continued, now citing Mawlana Khālid al-Baghdādī's *Ādāb al-ṭarīqat al-naqshbandiyya* (Proprieties of the Naqshbandi Sufi path): "As for the proprieties of being present with one's spiritual guide, they include refraining from looking at his face; bowing one's neck for him; standing before him the way the runaway slave who has been caught and brought to his master the Sultan does; refraining from sitting unless he commands it; refraining from initiating any talk that the sacred Law does not necessitate, or some danger on the road, or something of direct concern to the *murshid*; not to speak with those that are present there even if they are shaykhs and not to turn to them; rather, to **keep silent, close one's eyes and turn oneself inwardly with humble request for spiritual outpouring, counting him as a deputy for the Prophet–upon him the blessings and peace of Allah–and a Sultan in judgment and *taṣarruf* (discretionary power)**; and he sees all his interactions with him the same as his interaction with the Prophet–upon him the blessings and peace of Allah–and the Sultan. 'And when he intends to visit the Shaykh he does not reside with him more than a day and a night, and he does not busy himself with marital cohabitation for that breaks the blessing of his journey,' as stated in the *Iḥyā'*." He may reside for more than a day and night with other than the Shaykh if he comes from very far or if the Shaykh ordered him. All of the above is in fact subject to the Shaykh's preference.

He continued, "Also of the etiquette and manners of being in the presence of the Shaykh is that he never attends with a distracted heart, or a preoccupied heart, or an objection, or a test, or dislike. For all the above compels aversion from the *murshid*'s heart for the murid, so the latter might fall from the former's gaze and the Shaykh might even expel him from his heart. Falling from the seventh sky to the lowest earth would be preferable than falling out of the heart of the liege lords of inward states. So may Allah Most High protect us and you from that!" I.e. it is worse than the falling off of Iblis, for the latter fell from the nearest sky to the first earth. Think on it.

He continued, "So he has to **be sure to maintain full control of his *wuqūf qalbī* (heart's undivided attention), banishing heedlessness, pursuing inward outpourings, tying fast his heart with his heart in the sense of love and humble beseeching, watching and waiting for his turning to him, and being certain that the *fayḍ*** (spiritual outpouring) **of his *murshid* has filled the horizon completely, and that it depends only on the quest of the murid, even if the latter did not perceive it.**

فَلَا بُدَّ فِي الحُضُورِ مَعَهُ أَنْ يَكُونَ ضَابِطاً عَلَى الْوُقُوفِ الْقَلْبِيِّ، طَارِداً لِلْغَفْلَةِ، طَالِباً لِلْفَيْضِ الْبَاطِنِيِّ، رَابِطاً قَلْبَهُ بِقَلْبِهِ عَلَى وَجْهِ المَحَبَّةِ وَالتَّضَرُّعِ، مُنْتَظِراً لِتَوَجُّهِهِ وَالْتِفَاتِهِ وَمُوقِناً أَنَّ فَيْضَ مُرْشِدِهِ سَدَّ الْأُفُقِ وَمَلَأَ، وَمَوْقُوفٌ عَلَى طَلَبِ المُرِيدِ فَقَطْ، وَإِنْ لَمْ يُدْرِكْهُ

"For perceiving is not a precondition of attainment. Rather the precondition of the latter is pure conviction and genuine expectation of attainment. Furthermore, the people of the world do not harm the spiritual guide, and the search for the world is as one's own interest dictates. He should not stay too long with him lest his heart should dislike it – may Allah protect us from that – and he should not become preoccupied by the external appearance of the *murshid* away from his internal reality lest he become deprived of the inward outpouring. **For the external aspect of the *murshid* is for the people of externalities and his inward aspect is for the people of inward realities, and neither does creation distract him from the truth, nor does the truth distract him from creation. Rather all of the murids are in his heart like a mustard seed in the palm of his hand.**

"He must single out his Shaykh in the sense that there is no one on the face of the earth that can make him reach his nurturing Lord if not for him.

وَأَنْ يُفْرِدَ شَيْخَهُ بِمَعْنَى أَنَّهُ لَيْسَ عَلَى وَجْهِ الأَرْضِ
أَحَدٌ يُوصِلُهُ إِلَى رَبِّهِ لَوْلاهُ

"He must have fear and reverence towards his *murshid* with burning hope for his help and care, and he must be on guard against his Shaykh's punishment of him whether in his presence or in his absence. For Allah Most High lets him see the acts of the murids and their very steps, even if he does not let them realize it but rarely. He must not be deceived by the murshid's laughter and excellent manners with him outwardly. On the contrary he must hope to put an end to outward interaction with him – for to some of them he gives them the outward but deprives them of the inward – and he must never hope for the *murshid* to give him importance because the *murshid*'s magnification of the murid is a poison. It means he considers him an outsider. As for the *murshid*'s deprecation of the murid it is for his education, on top of the fact that there is never any lack of testing for the murid in all his acts and states." Our guide and our master Shaykh Hisham said, "There is no end to the testing of the murid even if he is a Shaykh. They crush you to a powder including the bones and then they crush the powder too."

Mawlana Shaykh Khālid continued: "And of the high manners is for the murid not to eat together with his Shaykh, and not to wear his clothes, and not to drink from his cup, and not to sit in his place, and not to ride on his ride unless he should command all of the above. He must not marry his spouse after his death, nor saddle up before he does, nor alight to camp before he does, nor sleep before he does is he is serving him, nor stand near his latrine when he goes there or where he could see him from in open space, and he does not pass his need in his latrine nor use what he used, all out of magnification for the *murshid*. Nor does he keep anything from him when he asks him, not even his sin, nor does he keep to himself even a fleeting thought in his heart when he is unable to suppress it through repentance and asking forgiveness, whether it is about the *murshid* or his way or the prohibitions that apply to himself. Rather he exposes them on the spot so that he will repel it from him, or else the door of outpouring will be closed shut as long as it remains in his heart.

"And he says nothing of his inner states to anyone other than the *murshid*. He shares them with the latter on the spot, and he loves whomever the latter loves and hates whomever the latter hates, and he forever keeps away from the people of reprehensible innovation, the possessors of heedlessness and the deniers. For the hardness of their hearts reflects back onto the heart of the murid, thereby extinguishing light just as water extinguishes fire, and its muddles his vigilant presence, and it results in heedlessness, hardness and inertia of the heart in the *dhikr* (remembrance), and it might even prevent him from the *dhikr* altogether. **He must not eat from the food of the deniers for it blocks up the door of spiritual outpouring for forty days.**

وَلَا يَأْكُلُ طَعَامَ الْمُنْكِرِينَ فَإِنَّهُ يَسُدُّ بَابَ الْفَيْضِ أَرْبَعِينَ يَوْماً

"Rather he eats the food of a sincere person which someone in a pure state of ablution has prepared—and if the latter is of the people of presence-of-heart then it is better. Nor does he have vehement eagerness for food and drink, nor does he eat out of greed and overfondness for eating, nor does he eat with an inattentive heart because **the morself of heedlessness bequeaths heedlessness and the morself of presence-of-heart bequeaths presence of heart**. He keeps his ego clear of anger and laughter for they both extinguish the light of *nisba* (spiritual affiliation) and they cause th heart to die. He speaks with the *murshid* with permission, lowering his voice, and he gives credence to whatever he says both with his heart and with his tongue, and he never counters it with 'No' and 'Why?' – neither verbally nor as a fleeting thought."

This is powerful advice and a crucial directive. Imam Qushayrī narrated in the *Risāla*, in the "Chapter on guarding the hearts of the masters and quitting disagreeing with them," from Ibn Fūrak, that the Imam of the Shāfi'īs in Khurāsān, Abū Sahl Muḥammad b. Sulaymān al-Ṣu'lūkī (d. 369/980) said, "Whoever says to his teacher, *lima?* (why?) will never prosper;" and from al-Qushayrī's own Shaykh, Abū 'Alī al-Daqqāq, "Whoever goes against his teacher is no longer on his path and the tie between the two of them has been severed even if they are together in the same place. So whoever kept company with one of the Shaykhs then objected to him in his heart has violated the covenant of companionship and repentance is due on him, although it has been said that there is no repentance for breaching the rights of teachers." Al-Qushayrī continued, in commentary of the saying of Allah on Mūsā's meeting with al-Khaḍir–upon them peace:

﴿ قَالَ لَهُۥ مُوسَىٰ هَلْ أَتَّبِعُكَ عَلَىٰٓ أَن تُعَلِّمَنِ مِمَّا عُلِّمْتَ رُشْدًا ﴿٦٦﴾ ﴾

الكهف

Mūsā said to him, "Shall I follow you provided you teach me from what you have been taught, upright guidance?" (al-Kahf 18:66): "When he wanted to keep company with al-Khaḍir he duly observed the prerequisite of manners and first asked permission to keep him company. Then al-Khaḍir made permission conditional upon not objecting to him in any decision. Thereafter, when Mūsā disagreed with him, he let it pass the first time and the second time. But when he did it a third time—three being the maximum definition of fewness and the minimum definition of multitude—he imposed upon him a parting of the ways, saying:

﴿ هَٰذَا فِرَاقُ بَيْنِي وَبَيْنِكَ ﴾ الكهف ٧٨

This is the parting of our mutual company (al-Kahf 18:78)." Al-ʿArūsī said in his commentary on the *Qushayriyya*, "I.e. as a disciplining of him and a direction to the paths of perfection with respect to the right due to the masters." Imam al-Qushayrī said in his *Laṭā'if al-ishārāt* on that verse, "For the murid has no right to say 'no' to his shaykh, nor does the student with his teacher, nor does the common person with the mufti in what the latter gives fatwa and decides."

Mawlāna Shaykh Khālid continued in his *Ādāb al-Ṭarīqat al-Naqshbandiyya*: "Nor may he ask from him any display of miraculous gift. Nor may he ask from him to change his *dhikr* to another one." Al-Quḥḥī cited all of the above and more in his book *Tanbīh al-sālikīn*.

IX
The visitations of Iraq, which is the kernel of the book

Of the famous visitations of Iraq are the resting-places of the following figures.

1. **The spiritual Pole of the knowers of Allah, the greatest arch-helper, Shaykh ʿAbd al-Qādir b. Abī Ṣāliḥ al-Jīlī**, also known as al-Gaylānī, and his two sons Shaykh ʿAbd al-Jabbār and Shaykh Ṣāliḥ–Allah sanctify their spirits. Shaykh ʿAbd al-Qādir was born in 470/1078 in one of the towns the province of Gaylān beyond Tabaristan and he died in Baghdad on the eighth night of Rabiʿ al-Ākhir 561/10 February 1166. Shaykh ʿAlī al-Shaṭṭanūfī al-Shāfiʿī penned his biography in his book *Bahjat al-asrār wa-maʿdin al-anwār fī manāqib al-sādat al-akhyār min al-mashāyikh al-abrār* (The beauty of secrets and the vessel of lights concerning the virtues of the elect masters of the pious shaykhs) and the Hadith master Ibn al-Mulaqqin has a long biography of the Shaykh which he mentioned in *Ṭabaqāt al-awliyāʾ* (Generation-layers of the Friends of Allah) and which he entitled *Durar al-jawāhir fī dhikri shayʾin min manāqib sayyidī ʿAbd al-Qādir* (The pearls of jewels consisting in the mention of some of the virtues of my master ʿAbd al-Qādir). The Tunisian Mālikī jurist, qadi and hadith scholar Muḥammad al-Makkī Ibn ʿAzzūz al-Ḥasanī (1270-1334/1854-1916) authored beneficial epistles on the Shaykh.

He is the Sayyid, Shaykh ʿAbd al-Qādir b. Mūsā b. ʿAbd Allāh b. Yaḥyā al-Zāhid b. Muḥammad b. Dāwūd b. Mūsā b. ʿAbd Allāh b. Mūsā al-Jawn b. ʿAbd Allāh al-Maḥḍ b. al-Ḥasan al-Muthannā b. al-Ḥasan b. ʿAlī b. Abī Ṭālib–may Allah be well-pleased with them. His resting-place is in the spot called Bab al-Shaykh on the eastern side of Baghdad. He studied and became one of the great ulema of the Ḥanbalīs then he kept complete isolation and seclusion, discipline and journeying, keeping vigil and hunger until he became one of the major Sufi masters. His shrine is the source of lights, the secrets of secrets and the alighting-place of tranquillity, blessing and majesty. Among his writings: *al-Ghunya li-ṭālibī ṭarīq al-Ḥaqq* (The sufficiency for the seekers of the way to the All-True), *Sirr al-asrār wa-maẓhar al-anwār fīmā yaḥtāju ilayhi al-abrār* (The secret of secrets and the manifestation of lights concerning what the pious need), *al-Fayḍ al-raḥmānī* (The outpouring from the All-Beneficent), *Futūḥ al-ghayb* (Openings from the unseen) and others.

Definition of the Sufi in the *Book of the manners of the murids*

Shaykh ʿAbd al-Qādir said in the "Book of the manners of the murids" in his *Ghunya*: "The *mutaṣawwif* (aspirant) tasks himself to carry while the Sufi is carried up. The former is made to carry everything heavy and light, so he carries until his ego melts away, his whim ceases to be and his will and hopes fade out so that he has become *ṣāfī* (pure) so he is then named Sufi. He carried, so he became aloft-worthy (or: carried by the decree), *karrat al-mashīʾa* (resilient-willed) (or *kurat al-mashīʾa*, the ball of divine will), *murabbā al-nafs* (discipline-souled) (or: *murabbā al-quds*, brought up by the All-Holy), the source of knowledges and wisdoms, the house of security and light, the cave of *awliyāʾ* and *abdāl* (substitute-*awliyāʾ*), their arrival and return (or: their conclusion and reference), their breathing space and rest, their elation! For he is the very necklace, the pearl of the diadem, the locus of the gaze of the nurturing Lord, whereas the *mutaṣawwif* murid is fighting himself to the death, his whim, his devil, his Lord's creation, his world and his hereafter, striving to worship his nurturing Lord in complete separation from the six directions and all things, by no longer working for their sake and in conformity with them and to gain their acceptance, by cleansing his inward self from inclination to them and any business with them. So he will contravene his devil and abandon his world, he will part ways with his contemporaries and the rest of his nurturing Lord's creation by His decision – He is almighty and exalted – for the pursuit of his hereafter, then he will struggle against his ego and his whim by the command of Allah almighty and exalted so that he will part ways with his hereafter and all that He has prepared for His Friends therein of gardens of Paradise because of sheer desire for his Protector. Then he will divest himself of the universes and become quit of originated objects, *yatajawhar* (he will turn into a gem) for the nurturing Lord of creatures, whereby all attachments, causes and means, spouses and children are severed from him. Then all the sides are blocked up for him and there opens up before him the Side of all sides and the Door of all doors, namely the good pleasure in the decree of the nurturing Lord of creatures and the nurturing Lord of all lords. There shall take effect in him the act of He Who knows all that was and all that is to come, the All-Aware of secrets and hidden-most things, of the motions of the limbs and what hearts and intentions conceal. Then, opposite this door, another door will be opened which is called the door of nearness to the King of all and the Judge of All. Then he shall be raised thence to the gatherings of familiarity. Then he shall be made to sit on the seat of pure monotheism. Then the veils shall be lifted from him and he shall enter the abode of *fardāniyya* (exalted solitary rank). Majesty and magnificence shall be unveiled to him. Once his sight falls on majesty and magnificence he remains without identity, annihilated to himself and to his own attributes, to his change and his might and his movements and his volition, to his yearnings and his world and his heareafter! He will become as a translucent glass vessel filled with pure water in which forms are discerned. Nothing rules over him but the decree, nothing originates his life but the command. He is extinct to himself and to his own share, existing for his Protecting Friend and His command. He does not ask for everlastingness because everlastingness is for existents, whereas he is like an infant who des not eat until it is fed and does not get dressed until it is dressed. He is in complete abandon and resignation. *And We are turning them over to the right side and to the left* (al-Kahf 18:18).

﴿ وَنُقَلِّبُهُمْ ذَاتَ ٱلْيَمِينِ وَذَاتَ ٱلشِّمَالِ ﴾ الكهف ١٨

He is one possessing existence among creatures with corporeality, yet utterly separate from them in acts and works and secrets and inner thoughts and intentions—at that time he is called a Sufi."

He continued: "As for his manners with his shaykh then it is required for him to refrain from contravening his shaykh in his company outwardly and to refrain from objecting to him inwardly. For the open rebellious sinner is devoid of manners and the one who is secretly objecting is asking for his wrath. Rather, let him ever be an opponent to himself on behalf of his shaykh, stopping his ego short and reprimanding it openly and inwardly for contravening him; and he often recites, *our nurturing Lord! Forgive us and our brothers that preceded us in faith, and do not put in our hearts any rancor towards those that believed. Our nurturing Lord! Verily You are Most Kind, Most Merciful* (al-Ḥashr 59:10).

﴿ رَبَّنَا ٱغْفِرْ لَنَا وَلِإِخْوَٰنِنَا ٱلَّذِينَ سَبَقُونَا بِٱلْإِيمَـٰنِ وَلَا تَجْعَلْ فِى قُلُوبِنَا غِلًّا لِّلَّذِينَ ءَامَنُوا۟ رَبَّنَآ إِنَّكَ رَءُوفٌ رَّحِيمٌ ﴾ الحشر

"And if anything appears from the Shaykh that is disliked in the sacred Law, let it be preferably interpreted away from that as the striking of a simile or as an allusion; and he does not make it explicit lest he make others averse to him thereby. And if he should happen to see any blemish in him he covers it up for him and he goes back to accuse himself while he interprets it for the Shaykh according to the sacred Law. If he cannot find an excuse for him according to the sacred Law he asks forgiveness for the Shaykh and supplicates on his behalf for his bring enabled success, knowledge, alertness, divine protection and care of what is sacred. He does not believe that he is infallible. He does not tell anyone about it. When he returns to him on another day or another hour he firmly believes that that has gone away, and that the Shaykh has been moved to that which is a higher level and was not kept in the previous state, but that was only a passing inattentiveness and a loss of ablution and an interval between two states, for every two states possess an interval and a return to the dispensations of the sacred Law and its permissivness and a departure from strictness and the tougher way, such as the vestibule between the rooms and the intermediary station between two stations: a termination of the first state and a tarrying at the threshold of the second state, and a move from one state of friendship with Allah to another, and the doffing of one *wilāya* and the donning of another which is higher and nobler. For every day they are in an increase in nearness to Allah Almighty."

He continued: "And when the Shaykh gets angry and frowns in to his face, or he seems to be turning away from him, he does not stop coming to him. Rather he searches out his inner state and what bad manners he might have shown with respect to the Shaykh, or neglect in regard to the command of Allah Almighty, whether refraining from obeying a command or doing something prohibited. Let him then ask forgiveness of his nurturing Lord, repent to Him, and resolve never to do it again. Then he apologizes to the Shaykh, humbles himself before him, blandishes him and endears himself to him by shunning any contravention of him in the future, and continues to accompany him with perseverance so that he will make him an intermediary and a means between himself and his nurturing Lord, a way and avenue by which he may reach Him, in the same way as someone that wants to enter to see the king with whom he has no previous acquaintance, whereby he must surely light upon one of his doorkeepers or one of his courtiers and intimates so that the latter will enlighten him as to the protocol that is required with the king and the custom that is followed with him. From him he learns the correct manners and the way by which to address him, and that which is appropriate of gifts and niceties the like of which are not already in his keep, and that of which an abundance is preferable. So let him come to the house by its door and not scale it in some other way whereby he would be blamed and humiliated. **Let him be certain that Allah Almighty has made it the established custom for there to be on earth Shaykh and murid; companion and one**

that is accompanied; follower and one that is followed, from the time of Ādam and so until the Resurrection comes."

وَلْيَتَحَقَّقْ بِأَنَّ اللهَ عَزَّ وَجَلَّ أَجْرَى الْعَادَةَ بِأَنْ يَكُونَ فِي الْأَرْضِ شَيْخٌ وَمُرِيدٌ، صَاحِبٌ وَمَصْحُوبٌ، تَابِعٌ وَمَتْبُوعٌ، مِنْ لَدُنْ آدَمَ إِلَى أَنْ تَقُومَ السَّاعَةُ.

He continued: "So the Shaykhs—they are the very path to Allah Almighty and the dedicated guides to it, and the door which one takes to get on it. So it is imperative for every murid of Allah Almighty to have a Shaykh according to what we have demonstrated, except in exceptionally rare cases. For it is possible that Allah might elect one of his servants and undertake his education and his protection from the devil and the foibles of the ego and whim, such as the Prophet Ibrāhīm and our Prophet Muḥammad–upon them the blessings and peace of Allah–and Uways al-Qaranī among the Friends of Allah, and others. So that cannot be denied; except that we have made clear that which is predominant, mostly the case, safest and best." The above is all from the "Book of the manners of the murids" in Shaykh ʿAbd al-Qādir's *al-Ghunya li-ṭālibī ṭarīq al-Ḥaqq* (The sufficiency for the seekers of the way to the All-True).

He also said in his book *Sirr al-asrār* (The secret of secrets), in the chapter on "the exposition of the outward and the inward seclusion:" "The primary goal of *taṣawwuf* is the *taṣfiya* (purification) of the heart from blameworthy traits and the subduing of the ego and control of whims so that they will not take it over. Whoever improves it with seclusion, discipline, silence and keeping to perpetual remembrance with will, love, repentance, sincerity and sound Sunni creed, following in the footsteps of the righteous early Muslims – the Companions and the Followers among the Shaykhs and the ulema that put their knowledge into practice – when the believer sits in seclusion with repentence and *talqīn* (spiritual instruction) together with the above-mentioned prerequisites, Allah Most High makes pure his knowledge and his works; He illuminates his heart; He softens his flesh; He purifies his tongue and all his senses from the outward and the inward; He elevates his deeds to His presence, accepts them and hears his supplication just as it is said, 'Allah hears him that praises Him,' i.e. He accepts his prayer and his laud and his beseeching; and He bestows His servant, in exchange of it, nearness to Him and high levels, as Allah Most High said, *unto Him ascend the pure word and the righteous deed—He elevates it* (Fāṭir 35:10).

﴿إِلَيْهِ يَصْعَدُ ٱلْكَلِمُ ٱلطَّيِّبُ وَٱلْعَمَلُ ٱلصَّٰلِحُ يَرْفَعُهُۥ﴾ فاطر ١٠

"So Allah elevates the knowledge and the works and the worker to His nearness and His mercy and His levels with forgiveness and good pleasure. And once these ranks are reached by the keeper of seclusion his heart becomes like the sea that never changes despite people's infliction of harms, as he said–upon him the blessings and peace of Allah, 'Be a sea that does not alter.' [Spoken by the early Muslims. Narrated by al-Khaṭīb in *Tārīkh Baghdād* from Abū al-Ḥusayn 'Alī al-Naṣībī who said, 'Abū al-Qāsim al-Junayd said to me, "Why do you not settle rather than travel for now? You have become too weak to continue travelling." I said, "O Abū al-Qāsim, the jurists did not differ about running water but only about still water." He said, "O Abū al-Ḥasan, when you are going to stand still then be an ocean and nothing will alter you."'] **So the chiefs of staff of ego will die in him just as Fir'awn and his House perished in the sea, and the sea was not spoiled. Thereafter the ship of the sacred Law shall be safely sailing on top of it, and his most pure spirit will be plunging to its depth so that he can reach the jewel of the truth and extract some of the pearl of spiritual knowledge and the coral of the hidden subtleties, as Allah Most High said, *from them emerge the pearl and the coral*** (al-Raḥmān 55:22).

﴿ يَخْرُجُ مِنْهُمَا ٱللُّؤْلُؤُ وَٱلْمَرْجَانُ ﴿٢٢﴾ ﴾ الرحمن

"For this ocean is given to whomever brings together the sea of the outward and the inward, after which there is no more corruption remaining in the ocean of the heart. His repentance will be most pure, his knowledge beneficial, his works righteous, he will not lean to forbidden things on purpose, and any inadvertence or forgetfulness will be forgiven through regret, asking forgiveness, and certainty."

Of the oddest curiosities is what Shaykh Yūsuf b. Ḥasan b. ʿAbd al-Hādī al-Ṣāliḥī narrated in his treatise entitled *Bad' al-ʿulqa bi-lubs al-khirqa* (Embarking on the road of connection by wearing the Sufi patch)—quoting from Ibn Nāṣir al-Dīn al-Dimashqī's *Iṭfā' ḥarqat al-ḥawba bi-ilbās khirqat al-tawba* (Extinguishing the burn of anxiety by wearing the patch of repentance)—Shaykh Aḥmad b. ʿAbd al-Ḥalīm b. Taymiyya al-Ḥarrānī's statement, "I have worn the patch of *taṣawwuf* in the lineage of a group of Shaykhs, among them Shaykh ʿAbd al-Qādir al-Jīlī, which is the most prestigious of the famous [Sufi] paths." Ibn ʿAbd al-Hādī also cites his statement in *al-Masā'il al-Tibrīziyya*, "I [=Ibn Taymiyya] wore Shaykh ʿAbd al-Qādir's blessed [Sufi] patch with none but two links between me and him." It is likely that this is precisely *al-Mas'ala fil-nisbati ilā al-khirqa* (Question on affiliating oneself to the [Sufi] patch) which was published as part of the eighth question of the *Jāmiʿ al-masā'il* (Collected questions) published in 1432/2011, although the printed text has nothing to do with the subject of the *khirqa* but is only prolix preliminaries typical of the author, so it appears that the rest of the reply was suppressed. The "two links" he meant are (i) a compound of Abū ʿUmar Ibn Qudāma (d. 607/1210) and Muwaffaq al-Dīn Ibn Qudāma (541-620/1147-1223) who both relatedly narrated from Shaykh ʿAbd al-Qādir; and (ii) Ibn Abī ʿUmar Ibn Qudāma (d. 682) who narrated from Abū ʿUmar and al-Muwaffaq and was a teacher to Ibn Taymiyya. The latter also has a partial commentary on Shaykh ʿAbd al-Qādir's Sufi discourses *Futūḥ al-ghayb* (Disclosures of the unseen) which is reproduced in his *Fatāwā kubrā*.

2. The resting-place of Maʿrūf al-Karkhī, namely Abū Maḥfūẓ Maʿrūf b. Fayrūz al-Karkhī (d. 200/816), one of the major *awliyā'*. His supplication was answered. He was teacher to al-Sarīy al-Saqaṭī and the friend of Dāwūd al-Ṭā'ī. Supplication is answered at Maʿrūf al-Karkhī's gravesite, which the early Muslims described as *al-tiryāq al-mujarrab* (the proven cure-all) as mentioned by the hadith masters al-Sulamī, Qushayrī, Ibn al-Jawzī, Ibn al-Mulaqqin, al-Dhahabī and others. The grave exudes light, tranquility and the fragrance of amber. It is narrated that he used to travel by night, circumambulate the House of Allah and then return to Baghdad in a single night, i.e. Allah had graced him with the reality of the folding up of time and space. His parents were Christians, then they became Muslims at his hand. He himself had become Muslim at the hand of ʿAlī b. Mūsā al-Riḍā then he became his doorkeeper. One day the Shīʿa rushed the door of ʿAlī b. Mūsā, breaking Maʿrūf's ribs in the process, after which he died as narrated by al-Sulamī in *Ṭabaqāt al-Ṣūfiyya* (The generation-layers of the Sufis).

The author of *Tārīkh ʿulamā' Baghdād fil-qarn al-rābiʿ ʿashar* (Biographical history of the 14th-century ulema of Baghdad) and *Naẓm al-durar fi rijāl al-qarn al-rābiʿ ʿashar* (The pearl necklace: the ulema of the 14th century), Yūnus al-Shaykh Ibrāhīm al-Sāmarrā'ī, related in his book *Marāqid Baghdād* (Famous graves of Baghdad) from Shukrī al-Ālūsī: "In the year 1310/1893 Ḥasan Bāshā the governor of Baghdad renovated the edifice, embellished the prayer space, and built a dome above Shaykh Maʿrūf's grave, which lies east of the prayer space in the direction of the qibla in a subterranean vault. The sarcophagus that is in the resting-place today is but on top of the vault exactly above the grave. This vault is very long—about twelve degrees in depth. The Shaykh's grotto has been standing and chronicled since the year 612/1215. It is so solid and beautiful that it is counted among the wonders of its kind." Sāmarrā'ī did not mention that there was also a well in the same grotto. We used it for our ablutions and we drank our fill of its sweet water.

Shaykh Maʿrūf al-Karkhī said, "**How numerous are the righteous but how few are the truthful among the righteous!**" He also said, "**When Allah wants goodness for a servant He opens up for him the door of works and he closes up for him the door of debate.**" He also said, "**It is a mark of Allah's hatred towards a servant that the latter should be seen busy with what is of no concern of his with regard to himself.**" He also said in his supplication, "**I seek refuge in You from a hope that prevents the best deed.**" He also said about the Friends of Allah, "**If there were anything of this world in their hearts not one prostration of theirs would be valid.**" Imam Aḥmad b. Ḥanbal said of him, "Is anything meant by 'knowledge' other than what Maʿrūf has reached?"

3. The resting-place of Sarīy al-Saqaṭī (d. 253/867), namely Abū al-Ḥasan Sarīy b. al-Mughallis, the scrupulously Godfearing who was well-known for taking only pure sustenance, the teacher of al-Junayd and his maternal uncle. He accompanied Maʿrūf al-Karkhī and narrated from the Imams of Hadith. His grave is in the Shālijiyya area in the middle of the cemetery known as al-Junayd's Cemetery. Al-Sulamī said, "al-Sarīy was the first in Baghdad to have spoken in the tongue of pure monotheism and the realities of states, the Imam and Shaykh of the Baghdadis in his time, to whom the majority of the second generation-layer of the prominent Shaykhs of Baghdad are affiliated." Al-Junayd said he never saw anyone more worshipful than him.

Among his sayings: "How can a work be light when Godfearingness accompanies it?" He also said, "**Your strongest deed is your overcoming of your own ego.**" He also said, "**Among the signs of beguilement is for one to be blind to the defects of his ego.**" He also said, "**Verily the ego indeed keeps one too busy to pay attention to others** (i.e. stand in judgment of others)." He also said, "**No merchant makes a profit that compares to his own soul.**" He defined the *mu-*

taṣawwif as "he whose light of knowledge does not extinguish the light of his scrupulous Godfearingness; he who does not discourse on the basis of inward insight about a type of knowledge that is thoroughly invalidated by the manifest locution of the Book; and he whom the miraculous gifts bestowed by Allah do not drive to rend the curtains of Allah's prohibitions." He also said, "Beware lest your lot be that you have famous praise and a covered-up defect." He also said of the narration of Hadith: "These are shackles."

4. The resting-place of Imam al-Junayd al-Baghdādī (222?-298/837?-911), namely Abū al-Qāsim al-Junayd b. Muḥammad al-Khazzāz al-Qawārīrī al-Nahāwandī al-Baghdādī, one of the paragons of ascetics. He followed the legal school of Abū Thawr, one of the companions of al-Shāfiʿī–may Allah be well-pleased with them–and kept company with his maternal uncle al-Sarīy, al-Ḥārith al-Muḥāsibī, Mūḥammad b. ʿAlī al-Qaṣṣāb and others. Al-Junayd said, "People affiliate me to al-Sarīy but my only teacher is this one," meaning al-Qaṣṣāb. he described the prayer-beads as "the means of our arrival to whatever we arrived at—we will never abandon it." He instructed his student before he died, "Keep company, after me, with whomever you trust with respect to Allah's secret in you. Meaning, flee all claimants and intruders." He was once asked about certainty and replied, "It is to leave what you see for what you do not see." He narrated from his maternal uncle al-Sarīy that the latter said to him, "Abū al-Qāsim! Make your grave your storehouse and forward to it as long as you can do it, so that when you enter the storehouse what you have forwarded will please you." Junayd also said, "**You cannot fulfill your duty until you first give up what is rightly yours, and none has strength to do that but a Prophet or a most truthful one.**" He also said, "Time that you have lost cannot be made up and there is nothing more precious than time." He also said, "**The knower of Allah is he that is never the prisoner of a glimpse of the eye or of a single utterance.**" He also said, "The purest part of this Umma are the Sufis." He also said, "You must guard high spiritual energy jealously, for such guarding is the preliminary to all [great] things." He was seen in sleep after his death saying,

"They came to nought, those allusions! They vanished, those phrases! They faded, those vestiges (or: those definitions)! And nothing has benefited us but some few humble prayer-cycles we used to pray in the pre-dawn." He also said, "The paths are all blocked for creatures except whoever closely followed in the footsteps of the Messenger–upon him the blessings and peace of Allah–and followed his Summa and kept close to his way: verily the paths of all good things are all open to such a one." He also said, "**Whoever has not memorized the Qur'ān and has not written the Hadith cannot be taken as a guide in this great matter because our knowledge is restricted to the Qur'ān and the Sunna**."

مَنْ لَمْ يَحْفَظِ الْقُرْآنَ وَلَمْ يَكْتُبِ الحَدِيثَ لَا يُقْتَدَى بِهِ فِي هٰذَا الأَمْرِ، لِأَنَّ
عِلْمَنَا مُقَيَّدٌ بِالْكِتَابِ وَالسُّنَّةِ

Yet one was witnessed denying the truth of the above rule and claiming that "it was pure *taqiyya* (dissimulation) and *mudārāt* (maneuver) in order to placate the ulema of externalities." But the matter is not as he claimed. On the contrary, it is as already mentioned under Sarīy al-Saqaṭī about the Sufi novice, that for one to doff the Sharī'a is divine beguilement, not a miraculous gift. It is the state of a zindiq, not *ḥaqīqa* (spiritual reality), as famously related from Imam Mālik: "Whoever acquires *taṣawwuf* without acquiring fiqh has become a zindiq; whoever acquires fiqh without acquiring *taṣawwuf* has become depraved; and whoever acquires both fiqh and *taṣawwuf* has reached certainty." Its equivalent is coming up as related from al-Shiblī. Al-Shāfi'i said:

فَقِيهاً وَصُوفِيّاً فَكُنْ لَيْسَ وَاحِداً؛ فَإِنِّي وَحَقِّ اللهِ إِيَّاكَ أَنْصَحُ
فَذٰلِكَ قَاسٍ لَمْ يَذُقْ قَلْبُهُ تُقىً؛ وَهٰذَا جَهُولٌ: كَيْفَ ذُو الجَهْلِ يَصْلُحُ؟

Be both a jurisprudent and a Sufi – never just one of the two.
Truly, by the right owed to Allah, I am advising you sincerely!
For the former is hardened, his heart tastes no Godwariness,
While the latter is ignorant – of what use is the ignorant?

5. The resting-place of Shaykh Maḥmūd Aḥmad al-Nuʿaymī al-Naqshbandī near al-Junayd and al-Saqaṭī. He is among those from whom Shaykh ʿAbd al-Qādir Ibn al-Māḥī al-Jaylī – may Allah preserve him – has taken knowledge. I could not find any biographical details of his.

6. The resting-place of the Prophet Yūshaʿ b. Nūn b. Afrāʾīm b. Yūsuf – upon them peace. Al-Ṭabarī and others narrated this genealogy from Ibn ʿAbbās, Qatāda, Suddī, and thus was it mentioned in the Book of Numbers. Muqātil said he was Mūsā's sororal nephew.

7. The resting-place of Shaykh Ibrāhīm al-Khawwāṣ (d. 291/904), namely Abū Isḥāq Ibrāhīm b. Aḥmad b. Ismāʿīl–Allah have mercy on him–the possessor of high stations in spiritual journeying and disciplines. There is a grave for him in Baghdad in al-Junayd's cemetery, however he died and was buried in al-Ray according to al-Sulamī, Ibn al-Mulaqqin and al-Shaʿrānī. Among his statements: "**The medication of the heart is five things: reading the Qurʾān with contemplation; keeping the stomach empty; standing in prayer in the dead of night; supplicating fervently in the pre-dawn; and sitting with the righteous.**" He also said, "Knowledge does not consist in abundant narration. Knowledge is only whoever follows knowledge, puts it into practice and complies obediently with the Sunnas even if one has little knowledge." I.e. knowledge according to the great Shaykhs is practice and wisdom; and whatever falls short of these two is not called knowledge, as documented in detail in the reports compiled by al-Khaṭīb al-Baghdādī–Allah have mercy on him–in his manual *Iqtiḍāʾ al-īlm al-ʿamal* (Knowledge positively requires practice). He also said, "I have read in the Torah: "Pity the son of Ādam! He commits a sin and he asks forgiveness of Me, so I forgive him. Then he does it again and he asks forgiveness of me, so I forgive him. Pity him! Neither he quits sinning nor does he despair of My mercy. I call you to witness, O my angels, that I have forgiven him." He was once asked, "How did you reach this rank?" He said, "By serving the poor."

8. The resting-place of Buhlūl al-Kūfī (d. 190/806), namely Abū Wuhayb Buhlūl b. ʿAmr al-Ṣayrafī al-Kūfī al-Baghdādī. Al-Khaṭīb in his *Tārīkh Baghdād* mentioned that Buhlūl was of the "mad sages." The Hadith master al-Rashīd al-ʿAṭṭār listed him among those that narrated from Mālik while Ibn Shākir al-Kutbī in *Fawāt al-wafayāt* added that "Hārūn al-Rashīd or some other caliph would make time for him to listen to what he might say." His grave is in the vicinity of al-Junayd's resting-place. Shaykh ʿAbd al-Qādir quoted some of his words in the *Ghunya*. He related: "Buhlūl al-Majnūn was asked, 'When is the servant truly relying on Allah?' He replied, 'When he is a stranger among people with his identity and someone near to the All-True with his heart.'"

Al-Dhahabī wrote of him in *Tārīkh al-Islām*: "His reason was affected by something but I do not think he became muddled or, at the very least, he would be fully cognizant at times. So he is counted among the sages of the madmen. He said some beautiful things and stories, and he narrated from ʿAmr b. Dīnār, ʿĀṣim b. Bahdala and Ayman b. Nā'il. They did not bring forward any commendation or discreditation of him [i.e. as a narrator of Hadith], nor did any student write anything from him. He lived in al-Rashīd's rule. Ibn al-Najjār wrote a long biographical entry on him [in *Dhayl Tārīkh Baghdād* (Supplement to al-Khaṭīb's History of Baghdad), which is lost but for the letter *ʿayn*] and he mentioned that he came to Baghdad. It is related from al-Aṣmaʿī that he said, 'I came out from al-Rashīd's presence through Bāb al-Ruṣafa and, behold, there was Buhlūl eating some *khabīṣ* (dates and ghee pudding). So I said to him, "Feed me some." He said, "It is not mine." I asked, "Whose is it?" He replied, "Ḥamdūna's, al-Rashīd's daughter. She gave it to me so that I would eat it on her behalf."' It was narrated from al-Ahshalī that he said, 'I went out early for some special need, whereupon I encountered Bahlūl, so I asked him to supplicate for me. He raised his hands and said, "O You without whom needs cannot be met, fulfill for me my needs in this life and the next." Upon hearing his supplication I felt at peace. Then I gave him two dirhams but he said to me, "Abū Muḥammad! You know that I would take a bread loaf and the like. No, by Allah! I would never take a fee for supplicating." Later my pressing need was fulfilled.' When Hārūn al-Rashīd ordered for some money to be given to him after he had admonished him he said, 'No! I will not stain the face of admonition.' Someone complained to him, 'Prices have gone up so supplicate to Allah.' He said, 'I do not care even if a seed will cost a dinar. Verily it rests upon us to worship Allah just as He commanded us and it rests upon Allah to provide for us just as He promised us.' Ḥasan b. Sahl narrated: 'I saw some boys throwing pebbles at al-Buhlūl and one pebble made him bleed, whereupon he said,

it may be even some thrower of hurtful stones at me
I'll yet find no recourse but feel protective of.

"'I said, "You feel protective of them as they are shooting at you?" He said, "Be quiet! perhaps Allah will see my distress and pain, and their great joy, so He will bestow us to one another."' It is also related from him that he said, "Whoever has the next life as his greatest concern, this life shall come to him despite itself." Then he said,

O proposer to this life in marriage, walk
away from proposing and you'll be safe.
Verily you propose to one most deceitful,
whose wedding's adjacent to its funeral meal!

"Abū al-Qāsim [al-Ḥasan b. Muḥammad b. Ḥabīb al-Naysābūrī (d. 406/1015] the commentator of the Qur'ān has related his stories and poetry in his book *'Uqalā' al-majānīn* (Sages of the madmen)."

The conclusion of the visitations of Baghdad the City of Peace will come after the next few sections *in shā' Allāh.*

9. In al-Madā'in we visited its chief grave, the resting place of the foremost horseman Salmān al-Fārisī–Allah be well-pleased with him (d. 32/653). He is also known as Salmān Ibn al-Islām (Salmān the son of submission) and Salmān al-Khayr (Salmān of goodness). His teknonym was Abū ʿAbd Allāh. He came from Rāmahurmuz. It was also said, Ispahan. He was a Zoroastrian who then converted to Christianity and migrated to Syro-Palestine where he resided for a while. He had heard that the Prophet–upon him the blessings and peace of Allah–would soon be sent so he went out in search of that. He came to the Hijaz and submitted in the fifth year of the Hijra (626). He was made prisoner and was sold in Medina where he worked as a slave. The Prophet–upon him the blessings and peace of Allah–paid for his freedom. His first battle was the Trench (5/627), at which time the Emigrants and the Helpers disagreed as to which of their respective groups he belonged with, whereupon the Prophet –upon him the blessings and peace of Allah–said, "**Salmān is one of us, the people of the House!**" as we narrated from Muḥyī al-Sunna Abū Muḥammad Mawlāna Shaykh Nazim al-Ḥaqqānī in *Musnad Ahl al-Bayt* through Abū Muḥammad Muḥyī al-Sunna al-Baghawī (433-516/ 1042-1122) and we clarified that it is a *ḥasan* (fair) hadith there. Salmān took part in the rest of the battles and the conquest of Iraq, and he was made governor of al-Madā'in.

Al-Ṣafīy said in *Rashaḥāt ʿayn al-ḥayāt* (Dewfalls from the source of life): "At the time that the Prophet–upon him the blessings and peace of Allah–had heard that the leagued forces were planning to attack, Salmān suggested to him to dig a trench on the borders of Medina. The Prophet took his advice and took part in the digging himself, seeking its reward and encouraging others. As Salmān was digging he struck upon a large rock which thwarted him as the Messenger of Allah–upon him the blessings and peace of Allah–was near him. The latter then took the pickaxe from Salmān's hand and struck the rock hard three times, splitting it on the third blow. Mūsā b. 'Uqba narrated in the *Maghāzī* and, through the latter, al-Bayhaqī in *Dalā'il al-Nubuwwa* that at that time Salmān al-Fārisī sighted, upon each blow of the Prophet's pickaxe, a flash of lightning that darted in a different direction each time, and each time Salmān would follow it with his eyes. He mentioned the event to the Messenger–upon him the blessings and peace of Allah. 'Messenger of Allah, I saw something like lightning or some surging wave of water at each strike that you struck, one going towards the east, another towards the north (or: Syro-Palestine) and another towards the south (or: Yemen).' The Prophet–upon him the blessings and peace of Allah–said, '**Have you really seen that, O Salmān?**' He said yes. The Prophet said, '**In the first of them the *Madā'in* (cities) of Kisrā and other cities of those regions were illuminated for me. In the next one the city of the Byzantines, and Syro-Palestine. In the latter one the city of Yemen and its palaces. That which I saw is help to victory reaching them, if Allah wills.**'"

رأيتُ كهيئة البرق أو موج الماء عن ضربة ضربتَها يا رسول الله، ذهبَت إحداهن نحو المشرق، والأخرى نحو الشام، والأخرى نحو اليَمَن. فقال النبي ﷺ: وَقَدْ رَأَيْتَ ذَلِكَ يَا سَلْمَانَ؟ قال: نعم، قد رأيت ذلك يا رسول الله. فقال رسول الله ﷺ:

فَإِنَّهُ ابْيَضَّ لِي فِي إِحْدَاهُنَّ مَدَائِنُ كِسْرَى وَمَدَائِنُ مِنْ تِلْكَ الْبِلَادِ، وَفِي الْأُخْرَى مَدِينَةُ الرُّومِ وَالشَّامِ، وَفِي الْأُخْرَى مَدِينَةُ الْيَمَنِ وَقُصُورِهَا، وَالَّذِي رَأَيْتُ: النَّصْرُ يَبْلُغُهُنَّ إِنْ شَاءَ اللهُ

Its paths and wordings are documented in the chapter on the Prophetic knowledge of the unseen from the arch-erudite Qadi Yūsuf al-

Nabhāni's book *Ḥujjatu-l-Lāh ʿalā al-ʿālamīn bi-muʿjizāt Sayyid al-mursalīn* (The conclusive proof of Allah over the worlds with the staggering miracles of the Master of Messengers) that was translated and published as *The Prophet's knowledge of the unseen.*

Mawlāna al-Ṣafīy continued in the *Rashaḥāt*: "What this hadith contains of glad tidings for the masters of subtle allusions is evident, to the effect that, in this spiritual path inherited from Salmān–Allah be well-pleased with him–arduous efforts, hardships and painful tests will be inevitable at the beginning, and great spiritual manifestation will come at the end, and spiritual conquests follow the latter. When the lands of non-Arabs (=Persia) were conquered and the armies of the Muslims took control of the Madā'in Kisrā, their governance was entrusted to Salmān al-Fārisī–Allah be well-pleased with him–which he took up to the end of his life. Yet he would only eat from the fruit of his own labor, even as the someone in command over thirty thousand Muslims and his yearly stipend was five thousand [dirhams]. He would address the people wearing a large woolen wrap which he also used to sit and sleep on. He had no house but would shelter in the shade wherever he happened to be. if he sent out the servant for some need he would knead the dough instead, saying, 'We will not ask of her two tasks at once.' He would not eat from the alms of people. More than that, he would not let a slave of his buy out his freedom unless the latter had some source of income, saying, 'Do you want to feed me the filth of people?' [It is narrated thus by al-Thaʿlabī while ʿAbd al-Razzāq, Ibn Abī Shayba, al-Ṭabarī and al-Bayhaqī narrated it from Ibn ʿUmar.] He would say, 'The Messenger of Allah–upon him the blessings and peace of Allah–took it from us as a covenant and he said, "**Let each one's budget be the same as the traveller's provision.**"'"

عَهِدَ إِلينا رسول الله ﷺ وقال: لِيَكُنْ بُلْغَةُ أَحَدِكُمْ مِثْلَ زَادِ الرَّاكِبِ

Narrated by Ibn Saʿd, Ibn Abī Shayba, Aḥmad, al-Ḥakim and others. He mentioned ity on his deathbed, weeping, as narrated by Hannād b.

Sarīy, Ibn al-Aʿrābī, Ibn Abī Shayba, Ibn Abī al-Dunyā in *al-Muḥtaḍarīn* (Book of the dying), Ibn Mājah, Abū Nuʿaym and al-Bayhaqī in the *Shuʿab*.

10. In al-Madāʾin also is found the grave of the Companion ʿAbd Allāh b. Jābir al-Anṣārī al-Bayāḍī-may Allah be well-pleased with him. The Hadith master Ibn Ḥajar said in the *Iṣāba*: "Bukhārī included him among the Prophetic Companions and Ibn Ḥibbān said he was indeed a Companion. Aḥmad narrated through Ibn ʿAqīl from ʿAbd Allāh b. Jābir that the latter said, 'I reached the Messenger of Allah–upon him the blessings and peace of Allah–as he had poured water, so I said, "Peace be upon you, Messenger of Allah!"' Al-Ṭabarānī, Ibn Abī ʿĀṣim and Ibn al-Sakan also narrated through ʿAbd Allāh b. Abī Sufyān al-Madanī from his grandfather [ʿUqba b. Abī ʿĀʾisha] that the latter said, 'I saw ʿAbd Allāh b. Jābir al-Bayāḍī the Companion of the Messenger of Allah–upon him the blessings and peace of Allah–with his forearms superposed in the prayer.'" The continuation of the hadith is that the Prophet said to Ibn Jābir al-Bayāḍī that **al-Fātiḥa is *khayru Sūratin fīl-Qurʾān* (the best Sura in the Qurʾān)**. It is also narrated by Abū Nuʿaym in *Maʿrifat al-Ṣaḥāba* and al-Bayhaqī in the *Shuʿab* with the addition, "**and it contains a cure for every ailment**." It was rated fair by al-Ḍiyāʾ al-Maqdisī, al-Haythamī and al-Suyūṭī.

أَلَا أُخْبِرُكَ يَا عَبْدَ اللهِ بْنَ جَابِرٍ بِأَخْيَرِ سُورَةٍ فِي الْقُرْآنِ؟ قلت: بلى يا رسول الله. قال: **اِقْرَأْ: ﴿ٱلْحَمْدُ لِلَّهِ رَبِّ ٱلْعَٰلَمِينَ﴾** حتّى ختمها. رواه أحمد بلفظ **بِخَيْرِ سُورَةٍ** وأبو نعيم في المعرفة والبيهقي في الشعب وقال: قال عليّ بن هاشم أحد رواته: **وَأَحْسَبُهُ قَالَ: فِيهَا شِفَاءٌ مِنْ كُلِّ دَاءٍ** وحسّنه الضياء المقدسي والهيثمي والسيوطي.

11. Also in al-Madā'in is the grave of Sayyid Ṭāhir b. Muḥammad al-Bāqir next to the grave of 'Abd Allāh b. Jābir al-Anṣārī. I could not find any biographical information on him. Then I found mentioned in one of the books of the Shī'īs "al-Sayyid Muḥammad Ṭāhir b. Muḥammad Bāqir al-Mūsawī the author of a Persian-language *Maqtal* (The Killing of...) which he excerpted from the contents of Abū Mikhnaf's *Maqtal*"—namely *Maqtal al-Ḥusayn* by the Shī'ī chronicler Abū Mikhnaf Lūṭ b. Yaḥyā b. Sa'īd b. Mikhnaf al-Azdī al-Kūfī—"in the year 1322/1904, and it was published then." Thus in Aghā Burug al-Tihrānī's *al-Dharī'a ilā taṣānīf al-Shī'a.*

12. Also in al-Madā'in is the grave of Ḥudhayfa b. al-Yamān the venerable Companion and son of a Companion–may Allah be well-pleased with both of them–the keeper of the secrets of the Messenger of Allah–upon him the blessings and peace of Allah. His father died as a shahid at Uḥud, after which he fought at the Battle of the Trench and his feats of prowess there are recorded. He narrated much from the Prophet–upon him the blessings and peace of Allah–and from him narrated the Companions and the Successors. Our liege lord 'Umar made him governor of al-Madā'in, where he died in the year 36/656, forty days after the killing of 'Uthmān (47bh-d. Jumu'a 18 Dhū al-Ḥijja 35/577-17 June 656) and the pledge to 'Alī–Allah be well-pleased with them. The Messenger of Allah–upon him the blessings and peace of Allah–exclusively entrusted him with knowledge of the seditions and the news of endtimes, among which a tremendous hadith concerning the proofs of Prophethood which Muslims narrated in his *Ṣaḥīḥ* wherein is mentioned the statement, "The Messenger of Allah–upon him be the blessings and peace of Allah–has certainly narrated to me what has taken place and what shall take place until the Hour rises." It is also mentioned in the two *Ṣaḥīḥ*s that Abū al-Dardā' said to 'Alqama the Successor, "Is there not among you [=Iraqis] the keeper of the secrets that none knows but he?" meaning Ḥudhayfa. It is also related in the two *Ṣaḥīḥ*s from 'Umar that he asked Ḥudahyfa about the Sedition. Ḥudhayfa took part in the battles of the conquest of Iraq and famous feats of prowess are arelated from him there. The above is mostly taken from Ibn Ḥajar's *al-Iṣāba fī Tamyīz al-Ṣaḥāba*.

13. In Wāsiṭ ("Middle" town i.e. between Kufa and Basra) we visited the grave of the venerable Successor **Abū Muḥammad Saʿīd b. Jubayr b. Hishām al-Asadī al-Wābilī**—*mawlāhum*—**al-Kūfī**, the Imam, Hadith master, transmitter of the Qur'ān and shahid student of Ibn ʿAbbās–Allah be well-pleased with them. He is among the giants of the Successors. He was heard repeating this verse in prayer twenty-odd times:

﴿ وَاتَّقُوا يَوْمًا تُرْجَعُونَ فِيهِ إِلَى اللَّهِ ثُمَّ تُوَفَّىٰ كُلُّ نَفْسٍ مَا كَسَبَتْ وَهُمْ لَا يُظْلَمُونَ ﴿٢٨١﴾ ﴾ البقرة

And beware a day on which you shall be brought back to the One God; then every soul shall be repaid in full whatever it has earned, and they shall not be wronged (al-Baqara 2:281).

It is narrated from Hilāl b. Yasāf that Saʿīd b. Jubayr entered the Kaʿba and recited the entire Qur'ān in one *rakʿa*. He entered the state of *iḥrām* twice a year: once for the Hajj and once for the ʿUmra. Among his sayings, "*Tawakkul* (reliance) on Allah is the *jimāʿ* of belief,"i.e. its sum total and most probable marker, the way it was said that "alcoholic drink is the *jimāʿ* of deliberate sin" (a Prophetic hadith related from Ibn Masʿūd, Abū al-Dardā', Zayd b. Khālid and ʿUqba b. ʿĀmir al-Juhanī). His habitual supplication was "O Allah, I am asking You the most beautiful reliance on You and the most beautiful opinion of You." He would say, "***Khashya* (awe) is for you to be in awe of Allah until your awe intervenes between you and your disobedience. That is true awe. As for *dhikr* it consists in obedience of Allah, so whoever obeys Allah has definitely remembered Him and whoever has not obeyed Him then such a person is certainly not a remem-**

berer of Him even if he makes much *tasbīḥ* and recitation of the Qur'ān!" He also said, "Do not put out your candles during the Ten Nights (Fajr 89:2, i.e. the first ten of Dhū-l-Ḥijja)." Worship pleased him. He wept much at night until he lost half his sight. He would say, "If the remembrance of death left my heart for a moment I would fear that my heart had become corrupt in me." Al-Ḥajjāj murdered him so he died as a shahid. May Allah be well-pleased with him and make him pleased.

14. In Umm ʿAbīda—in the Baṭā'iḥ district—we visited the resting-place of the Master of the Sufi Folk **Imam Aḥmad al-Rifāʿī al-Kabīr** (500-578/1107-1182). His full name is Abū al-ʿAbbās Aḥmad b. ʿAlī b. Yaḥyā al-Ḥusaynī. He hailed from the Maghreb and was a Shāfiʿī jurist and *muḥaddith*. The Baṭā'iḥ (plains) are a cluster of towns between Wāsiṭ and Basra. Among al-Rifāʿī's miraculous gifts is that the one afar could hear his voice like the one that was near him in the gathering and the deaf would attend his gathering, whereupon Allah would make them hear so that they could benefit from what he said. He was a wonder of humbleness. He named himself al-Lāshay' Uḥaymid (the nothing, little Ahmad) and *gharīb al-ghurabā'* (the stranger to strangers) and *shaykh man lā shaykha lah* (the shaykh of whoever has no shaykh).

Among his statements recorded in Ibn al-Mulaqqin's *Ṭabaqāt al-awliyā'*: "Whoever busies himself with what is of no concern or benefit to him will miss what is." "Taking comfort in the company of creatures is a severance from the All-True." "High manners are the way of life of the poor and the inheritance of the rich." Asked why the answer to the supplication gets barred he replied, "Dut to the scantiness of the halal." Asked about *futuwwa* he said, "It is to disregard the slips of your brethren and not see yourself as better than others." Asked about *taṣawwuf*, he replied, "Ours or yours?" The questioner said, "My master, it was one question and has become two? Explain them to me." He said, "Your *taṣawwuf* consists in your secret states to be pure, news of you to be wholesome, for you to obey your Almighty Lord, stand your night in prayer and fast your day. As for the *taṣawwuf* of the Folk then it is, as it was said:

Taṣawwuf is not to wear rags: whoever says so has deviated.
Verily taṣawwuf, young man, is a burning mixed with anguish.

It is said that he made his companions swear that if they ever saw any blemish in him they must notify him of it. Shaykh ʿUmar al-Fārūqī then said, "My master, I know of one blemish in you." He said, "And what is it?" He said, "My master, your blemish is that we are among your companions." The Shaykh wept and the *fuqarā'* wept. He said, "Aye, ʿUmar! If the bark is fit, it shall carry those on board." A plate of dates was set before him so he kept choosing the spoiled ones and eating them, saying, "I am the most deserving of the lesser stuff because I am just like it." He would not get up for the presidents and he would say, "Looking at their faces hardens the heart." His [last] illness was diarrhea which lasted for more than a month. It made him go to stool more than thirty times in a day and night, after each of which he would make a full ablution and pray. **He was asked to define the *mutamakkin* (possessor of *tamkīn*, firmness)[2] and he said, "He is the one that, if a fiery smoke were set before him on the highest summit of the earth with the southern winds storming, it would not move a single hair of his."**

وَسُئِلَ عَنْ وَصْفِ الْمُتَمَكِّنِ، فَقَالَ: هُوَ الَّذِي لَوْ نُصِبَ لَهُ سَنْسَانٌ - دُخانُ نَارٍ - عَلَى أَعْلَى شَاهِقٍ فِي الْأَرْضِ، وَهَبَّتِ الرِّيَاحُ الْيَمَانِيَّةُ، مَا حَرَّكَتْ مِنْهُ شَعْرَةً وَاحِدَةً

To a man who came to bid him farewell before leaving for Baghdad he said, "When you enter Baghdad do not visit anyone alive or dead before you visit Shaykh ʿAbd al-Qādir, for he has received the

[2] Mawlana Shaykh Nazim used this term to describe Shaykh Hisham.

promise that if any of the possessors of states that enters Baghdad does not visit him, his state will be removed from him even before his last breath."

He also said: "The writing of the Muhammadan Name is extended on the records of all the universes from the mother of the fringe of pre-existence—i.e. its inwardness and everything on its fringes—to the margin of the aftermath of everlastingness. And to its authority belongs the eternal conclusive proof that stands over every authority in existence." Thus in *Bawāriq al-ḥaqq* (The lightning flashes of the truth) by the knower Muḥammad Mahdī al-Ṣayyādī al-Rawwās.

15. Back in Baghdad, also among the famed visitations is the grave of **Sayyid Ahmad al-Rifāʿī's father**, namely Abū al-Ḥasan al-Sulṭān ʿAlī b. Yaḥyā (459-519/1067-1125)–may Allah have mercy on him–in the square on al-Rashīd street. His father, Sayyid Yaḥyā, was the chief of the descendants of Abū Ṭālib the paternal uncle of the Prophet–upon him the blessings and peace of Allah–in Basra where he had emigrated from the Maghreb and died. Shaykh Yūnus al-Sāmarrāʾī said in *Maraqid Baghdād* (The resting-places of Baghdad): "He (=ʿAlī b. Yaḥyā) was nicknamed *Sulṭān al-ʿārifīn* due to his mass-transmitted station and miraculous gifts and he married Fāṭima al-Anṣāriyya who bore him al-Sayyid Aḥmad al-Kabīr, al-Sayyid ʿUthmān, al-Sayyid Ismāʿīl and al-Sayyida Sitt al-Nasab. Al-Sayyid Muḥammad Abū al-Hudā b. Ḥasan Hādī b. ʿAlī al-Ṣayyādī authored a large book on his life and merits entitled *al-Nūr al-jalī fī akhbār wālid al-Imām al-Rifāʿī al-Sayyid Sulṭān ʿAlī* (The resplendent light on the news of Imam al-Rifāʿī's father Sultan ʿAlī). He was mentioned in Sayyid Aḥmad al-Rifāʿī's own book *Ḥālat ahl al-ḥaqīqa maʿa Allāh* (The special state of the people of spiritual reality with Allah) and other books. He has a magnificent status in the hearts of the righteous."

16. Sayyid Muḥammad Bahāʾ al-Dīn Mahdī al-Ṣayyādī al-Rifāʿī, famed as al-Rawwās (1220-1326/1805-1908) lies next to Sayyid Sultan ʿAlī–may Allah be well-pleased with them–and is known as the second

Rifāʿī. He is a descendant of al-Sayyid al-Rifāʿī as well as of Shaykh ʿAbd al-Qādir. Shaykh Yūnus al-Sāmarrāʾī said in *Marāqid Baghdād*: "He was born in the district of Sūq al-Shuyūkh in Baghdad and was orphaned of his father and mother in his young age. He memorized the Noble Qurʾān and studied the Islamic sciences then went on pilgrimage and stayed in Mecca for two years. Then he visited the Prophet–upon him the blessings and peace of Allah–and stayed in Medina for a year. He thus took learning from the ulema of the two Holy Sanctuaries. After that he went to Egypt and took up residence in al-Azhar al-Sharīf for 13 years receiving the sciences until he excelled in them. He connected with al-Amīr al-Kabīr (1154-1232/1741-1817) and Shaykh Thuʿaylib (or Thuʿaylīb) (1151-1239/1738-1824) and narrates from both according to what Sayyid Muḥammad Abū al-Hudā al-Ṣayyādī said in his book *Wasīlat al-ʿārifīn fī akhbār Bahāʾ al-Dīn al-Rawwās* (The knowers' means concerning the news of Bahāʾ al-Dīn al-Rawwās). Then he travelled with the caravan to Iraq where he met with the knower al-Sayyid ʿAbd Allāh al-Rāwī al-Rifāʿī from whom he took the Tariqa. After that he began his spiritual journeying, travelling to India, Khurasan and the non-Arab lands (=Persia), Kurdish lands, the Arabian peninsula and Anatolia, staying in each place no more than three months. Then he came back to Baghdad. He sustained himself from the work of his hands and sell the grilled heads of sheep and goats until he acquired the nickname of al-Rawwās (merchant of heads).

Among his works are *Fadhlakat al-ḥaqīqa* (The epitome of spiritual reality) which consists of 313 entries, the first of which being, "Embracing the convictions which the righteous predecessors of the people of the Sunna and the Congregation embraced and conformed with the massive majority of the imams of the faith, following one of the four famous Imams." The last is, "Sacrificing wealth and life in Allah as a sale pledged for Allah Most High." Also among them is *al-Durrat al-bayḍāʾ* (The white pearl), with chapters on the rulings of pure monotheism and tariqa, the recognition of the immense status of the Prophet–upon him the blessings and peace of Allah, putting together the two sourcings of the the practicing scholars and the gnostic shaykhs; the definition of the types of the friends of Allah, the definition of the spiritual specialty that is poured into some of the elite, and a conclusion with some delicate points of spiritual wisdom beginning with the statement, "Do not take up a position in which the tongue of the All-True will say to you: 'I am not with you.'" Also among them is *Barqamat al-bulbul* (The nightingale's warbling) which comprises some of al-Rawwās's miraculous gifts and his *hawātif* (spiritual calls). Also among them is *al-Ḥikam al-mahdawiyya al-multaqaṭa min durar al-imdādāt al-Nabawiyya* (The Mahdian wisdoms collected from the pearls of the Prophetic supplies), in which there is elevated discourse about the spiritual realities and divine Attributes according to the school of the people of the Sunna and the Congregation. Also among them is *Ṭay al-sijill* (The folding of the scroll), a very precious large book on *taṣawwuf*, the transmission chains of the tariqas and the Rifāʿī disciplines, realities and wisdoms. Also among them is *Bawāriq al-ḥaqā'iq* (The lightning flashes of the spiritual realities) which we already mentioned. It consists in the biography of the Shaykh, the mention of his travels and spiritual unveilings and states, and his 109 *bayʿa* (pledges) which he pledged to Sayyid Aḥmad al-Rifāʿī al-Kabīr in the *ḥaḍra ghaybiyya* (invisible spiritual presence). It resembles al-Shaʿrānī's *al-ʿUhūd al-Muḥammadiyya* (The Muhammadan pacts) in arrangement and style and it contains, among other matters, a magnificent invocation of blessings on the Prophet–upon him the blessings and peace of Allah–after seeing him in dream telling him, "Invoke blessings on me with an invocation that gathers all the goals of those of the people of the *ḥaḍra* that invoke blessings on me." I have all of the above works as edited by Shaykh ʿAbd al-Ḥakīm ʿAbd al-Bāsiṭ al-Saqbānī–may Allah have mercy on him.

17. Among the visitations of Baghdad is the grave of Imam Abū Ḥanīfa al-Nuʿmān b. Thābit al-Taymī—*mawlāhum* (by alliance)—(d. 150/767) –Allah be well-pleased with him. It is found in Jāmiʿ al-Imām in the Aʿẓamiyya quarter on the eastern side of Baghdad. It is mentioned in *Marāqid Baghdād* that this mosque is considered one of the most important old historical monuments of Baghdad and that its edifice and embellishment were renovated in the eighties and after that. Abū Ḥanīfa is the one about whom Imam al-Shāfi'ī said–Allah have mercy on them: "People are all the dependants of Abū Ḥanīfa in fiqh." Many of the imams of the early generations followed him and his school was codified by major mujtahids. It has mustered acceptance far and wide on earth until it became the school with the most followers among the four Sunni schools, especially in the Indian Subcontinent, central Asia and Turkey, and now in the US and Europe as well. May Allah reward him on behalf of the Umma. Al-Khaṭīb al-Baghdādī narrated in *Tārīkh Baghdad* with his chain to al-Shāfi'ī that the latter would come to the resting-place of Abū Ḥanīfa in Baghdad and pray two cycles of prayer then he would supplicate for the fulfillment of his need, and it would be answered because of the blessing of this station. Imam Abū Ḥanīfa was one of the signs of Allah in knowledge, intelligence, high manners and worshipfulness. He was nicknamed *al-watad* (the pillar) for standing in prayer so long and is counted—together with 'Uthmān b. 'Affān, Tamīm al-Dārī and Sa'īd b. Jubayr—among those who recited the entire Qur'ān in a single *rak'a*.

18. Among the visitations of Baghdad is also the grave of Abū Bakr al-Shiblī, namely Abū Bakr Dulaf b. Jaḥdar al-Khurāsānī al-Mālikī (d. 334/946). He was also known as Ja'far b. Yūnus. Al-Khaṭīb said he was the peerless one of his time in knowledge, the son of the chief chamberlain in the palace and his maternal uncle was the governor of Alexandria. He was an accomplished poet and his *Dīwān* is in print. He said in it:

If You had been for me a yearly feast,
then what would I do with the yearly feast?
Your love runs through my very heart
the way the water runs through the bough.

He accompanied al-Junayd and his generation. Ibn al-Mulaqqin said, "His self-discipline is mass-transmitted and **he greatly emphasized the magnification of the noble sacred Law**. His grave is near the mosque of Imam Abū Ḥanīfa. Among the words related from him he said, in explanation of the hadith,

خَيْرُ كَسْبِ الْمَرْءِ عَمَلُ يَمِينِهِ

"**One's best earning is the work of one's right hand**" [Aḥmad from Abū Hurayra]: "When night comes, take water and prepare for prayer and pray as much you want, and stretch out your hand and ask Allah: that is the earning of your right hand." He also said about the meaning of His statement–exalted is He–

﴿ قُل لِّلْمُؤْمِنِينَ يَغُضُّوا مِنْ أَبْصَٰرِهِمْ وَيَحْفَظُوا فُرُوجَهُمْ ۚ ذَٰلِكَ أَزْكَىٰ لَهُمْ ۗ إِنَّ ٱللَّهَ خَبِيرٌۢ بِمَا يَصْنَعُونَ ﴿٣٠﴾ ﴾ [النور]:

Tell the believers they must lower some of their gazes and guard their private parts. That is more wholesome for them. Verily the One God is All-Aware of what they make (al-Nūr 24:30): "Avert the gazes of the heads from forbidden things and the gazes of the hearts from other than Allah." He also said, "How much do people need an intoxication that makes them oblivious to their own egos and their acts and their states!" It may be the same meaning as al-Harawī al-Anṣārī's statement, *al-zuhd ʿani-l-zuhd* (doing without doing without) which one of the commentators of his *Manāzil al-sā'irīn* (The stations of the spiritual wayfarers) could not understand, so he commented, "This statement of his needs reconsideration. How can one do without doing without?"

Abū Bakr al-Shiblī declaimed:

you may reckon I am alive yet verily I am dead,
and part of me mourns the parting with the other.

and he said:

and whence can I say, "Where?" when verily, as you see,
I live without a heart and go about without a goal?

He also said, "**I know someone who did not embark into this great affair**—i.e. *taṣawwuf*—**until he had first spent all his property and drowned into this Tigris that you see seventy satchels filled with written notes, and memorized the *Muwaṭṭa'*, and recited [the Qur'ān] in this reading and that reading**!" meaning himself.

19. Also among the visitations of Baghdad is the grave of the Quṭb Bishr al-Ḥāfī, namely Abū Naṣr Bishr b. al-Ḥārith b. ʿAbd al-Raḥmān al-Marwazī (152-227/769-842)—Allah be well-pleased with him—the model of simple living, the Shaykh al-Islām and companion of al-Fuḍayl b. ʿIyāḍ. He took hadith from Ḥammad b. Zayd, ʿAbd Allāh b. al-Mubārak, Hushaym b. Bashīr, Abū Yūsuf the Qadi, Ibn ʿUlayya and others. His grave is in al-Aʿẓamiyya. He travelled in quest of knowledge to Mecca, Kufa and Basra and he narrated much hadith, except that he did not forward himself for narration. On the contrary he hated it and he buried his books because of that and turned to worship instead. So everything that was heard from him—as al-Khaṭīb stated—was only by way of *mudhākara* (reminder). He followed the school of Sufyān al-Thawrī in fiqh and *waraʿ* (scrupulous Godfearingness), contrary to the claim of the author of *Marāqid Baghdād* to the effect that Bish was a Ḥanafī. He was a friend of Imam Aḥmad whom he praised for his stance during the ordeal of the "creation of the Qur'ān" controversy, whereupon Aḥmad said, "Praise be to Allah Who has made Bishr pleased with what we have done." Bishr said, "Aḥmad was made superior to me in three things: pursuing the halal for himself and for others, whereas I pursue it for myself; bearing with marriage, whereas I cannot; and he has been made an imam for everyone, whereas I am pursuing solitariness for myself." As for Aḥmad he would describe Bishr as peerless in his time other than for 'Āmir b. 'Abd Qays, and he would say, "Would that we were left! The way is what Bishr b. al-Ḥārith followed." By being left he meant "left without reckoning," and Allah knows best. However, Aḥmad never stopped taking Bishr to task for not marrying and he would say, "Had he married it would have been complete for him."

Among the sayings of Bishr b. al-Ḥārith: "The most trusted of my deeds to me is love of the Companions of Muḥammad–upon him the blessings and peace of Allah." "I do not know any deed better than the pursuit of Hadith for whoever guards himself from Allah and whose intention is excellent in so doing." Yet he used to ask Allah forgiveness for pursuing Hadith. "You will not find the sweetness of worship until you put between yourself and appetites an iron wall." "It is enough for you that there are dead people whose remembrance revives the hearts, and there are living people whose sight hardens the hearts." He said upon entering the Bāb Ḥarb cemetery, "The dead within this wall are more numerous than those outside the wall." "The punishment of the learned scholar in this world is for his heart's heart to go blind," and in Allah is the refuge!

The reason Bishr buried his books of hadith is not as Imam al-Dhahabī claimed in his *Siyar*—and Allah knows best—namely that (i) it was for fear that some unscrupulous hadith scholar might tamper with them or add to them, whereby such would then be attributed to him, or that (ii) his sources in them were broken-chained and flimsy reports. Rather, the reason is that Bishr was too scrupulous about hadith narration and audition devoid of practice, exactly as he himself and his Imam Sufyān al-Thawrī explicitly stated—Allah be well-pleased with them. Bishr said to the scholars of hadith, "Remit the zakat of this Hadith! Put into practice, out of every 200 hadiths, [at least] five hadiths!" It is as Shaykh Abū al-Fatḥ al-Ghazālī said–Allah have mercy on him–"As for preaching I do not see myself qualified for it, because the minimum zakatable amount of preaching is the practice of what one preaches, and whoever has no minimum of that, how can he adduce the zakat itself? And can the shadow ever be straight when the stick is crooked?" Thus in *Ṭabaqāt al-awliyā'*. Bishr also said, "I ask forgiveness of Allah that at the mention of the chain of transmission there is pride in the heart." "Verily I crave narrating hadith and when I crave something I leave it." "**Hadith is not part of the preparation for death**." The same is related from Sufyān al-Thawrī. I.e. the mere audition and narration of hadith and its chain of transmission and its *ijāza* (certification) never suffice instead of the obligation of sincerity in repentance and the upbringing of the soul at the hand of the spiritual guide. The same is also related as spoken by Shaykh 'Abd al-Qādir al-Jaylānī to Shaykh Shihāb al-Dīn al-Suhrawardī about *uṣūl al-dīn* (credal doctrine) before the latter had even revealed to the former that he was thinking of writing about it: "O 'Umar! It is not part of the preparation for the grave."

Bishr lived with his sister. When she died he said, "When the servant falls short in obedience of Allah, Allah takes away from him the one from whose company he draws comfort." Imam Abū Ḥafṣ al-Suhrawardī commented on this statement in *'Awārif al-ma'ārif* (Signposts of the spiritual insights), in chapter 53 entitled *ḥaqīqat al-ṣuḥba* (The reality of companionship) saying: "Allah arranges *uns* (familiarity) for the truthful ones as a gentle gesture from Allah Most High and a reward in advance for the servant. The *anīs* (familiar companion) might be benefiting others like the Shaykhs do, and it might be the one benefiting like the murids do. The sound seclusion and isolation is not left without an *anīs*. If one is falling short, Allah will give him an *anīs* by whom his state will be completed. If he is not falling short, Allah shall put at his disposal whoever he draws comfort from among the murids. This *uns* does not entail inclination of the more general sort; rather it is with Allah, from Allah and in Allah."

20. Also among the visitations of Baghdad is the grave of Mūsā al-Kāẓim b. Ja'far al-Ṣādiq (128-183/746-799). He is sayyid Mūsā, the tamer of anger, the gentle one, the model guide, Abal-Ḥasan al-'Alawī, the father of ʿAlī b. Mūsā al-Riḍā–may Allah be well-pleased with them. He is a Medinan who resided in Baghdad. He narrated from his father and from him narrated his children and his two brothers. He was nicknamed *al-ʿabd al-ṣāliḥ* (the righteous servant) because of his worshipfulness and ijtihad. Al-Khaṭīb said, "Our colleagues narrated that he entered the mosque of the Messenger of Allah–upon him the blessings and peace of Allah–after which he went into a prostration early in the night in which he was heard saying, *ʿaẓīmu al-dhanbi ʿindī, fal-yaḥsuni al-ʿafwu ʿindak, yā ahl al-taqwā wa-yā ahl al-maghfira* (enormous sin is what I have, so let pardon be what You have, O Giver of godfearingness and Giver of forgiveness), and he went on repeating it until the dawn. He was most giving and generous. News might reach him that a certain man was speaking ill of him, whereupon he would send him a pouch containing a thousand gold pieces. He would parcel out pouches with three hundred dinars, four hundred dinars and two hundred dinars, then he would distribute them in Medina.

Shaykh Yūnus al-Sāmarrāʾī wrote in *Marāqid Baghdād*, "The Kāẓimiyya cemetery used to be known as the Graves of the Quraysh because the Caliph Abū Jaʿfar al-Manṣūr (d. 158/775), the founder of Madīnat al-Salām (the City of Peace=Baghdad), had taken this pot as a cemetery for the Qurashīs and their followers. His son was buried there and so was Umm Jaʿfar Zubayda, al-Amīn's mother. When Mūsā al-Kāẓim's grandson Abū Jaʿfar Muḥammad b. ʿAlī al-Jawwād died in the year 220/835 he was buried next to his grandfather in the known burial-place and it was dubbed *mashhad al-jawwādayn* (burial-place of the two generous ones). The whole area surrounding the burial-place northwest of Baghdad was affiliated to al-Kāẓim and so it was called al-Kāẓimiyya.

21. Also among the visitations of Baghdad is the grave of Imam Aḥmad b. Muḥammad b. Ḥanbal al-Marwazī al-Shaybānī (164-241/781-855)–Allah be well-pleased with him–the Imam of *Ahl al-Sunna wal-Jamāʿa*, the Seal of the major jurist Imams and their paramount expert in Hadith. The author of *Marāqid Baghdād* said his grave is in the Agha Mosque located near the Jumuʿa mosque of Ḥasan Bāshā in the Ḥaydar Khāna neighborhood and it bears an inscription stating it is the grave of Imam Aḥmad b. Ḥanbal. What is well-known, however, is that Imam Aḥmad was buried in the cemetery of Bāb Ḥarb in the western part of Baghdad together with Bishr al-Ḥāfī, Manṣūr b. ʿAmmār, al-Ḥusayn b. ʿAlī al-Khiraqī and others as mentioned by al-Khaṭīb in his *Tārīkh*, Yāqūt al-Ḥamawī in *Muʿjam al-buldān* and Ibn al-Jawzī in *al-Muntaẓam*. He continues saying that when his grave fell into the Tigris in 1937 because of a flood his remains were supposedly transported to the ʿĀrif Aghā mosque, for which there is no evidence–and Allah knows best.

Imam Aḥmad loved the Sufis and gave them special treatment as was already alluded to in the entries on Maʿrūf al-Karkhī and Bishr al-Ḥāfī. He would make them sit near him when they attended his gathering, as in the anecdote about Abū Ḥamza al-Ṣūfī—namely Muḥammad b. Ibrāhīm al-Khurāsānī (d. 290/903) who said, "Aḥmad would ask me about certain issues in his gathering and he would say, 'What do you say regarding it, O Sufi?'" Al-Khaṭīb narrated it in his *Tārīkh*. It is narrated in al-Sulamī's *Ṭabaqāt al-ṣūfiyya* and Ibn al-Mulaqqin's *Ṭabaqāt al-awliyā'* that Abū Ḥamza said, "Whoever takes to heart the remembrance of death, everything that abides forever becomes lovely to him and everything that passes away becomes hateful to him." Imam Aḥmad once said playfully to Yūsuf b. Ḥusayn al-Rāzī, "What will you do with Hadith, O Sufi?" Then he narrated to him from Anas–Allah be well-pleased with him–that the Messenger of Allah–upon him the blessings and peace of Allah–said, "**O Bilal! Do not feel penury from the Owner of the Throne. Verily Allah shall bring the provision of every morrow**."

يَا بِلَالُ، لَا تَخَفْ مِنْ ذِي الْعَرْشِ إِقْلَالاً، إِنَّ اللهَ يَأْتِي بِرِزْقِ كُلِّ غَدٍ

The Hadith master al-Mālīnī—al-Khaṭīb's teacher—narrated it in his *Forty hadiths through the Sufi masters* as well as Ibn Abī Shayba, Abū

Nu'aym and al-Khaṭīb himself. It was also narrated from Abū Hurayra by al-Bazzār and al-Ṭabarānī and from other Companions.

22. Also among the visitations of Baghdad is the grave of his son 'Abd Allāh b. Aḥmad b. Ḥanbal—who narrated the *Musnad* from him—in the Qaṭī'at Umm Ja'far near the Benzine Khānat al-Kāẓimiyya on al-Muḥīṭ street. Al-Khaṭīb in *Tārīkh Baghdād* and Ibn Abī Ya'lā in *Ṭabaqāt al-Ḥanābila* both narrated that 'Abd Allāh instructed that he should be buried there. When asked why, he said he had veracious evidence that there was a Prophet buried there "and I prefer to be buried near a Prophet than near my father."

23. Also among the visitations of Baghdad is the grave of al-Ḥārith al-Muḥāsibī (d. 243/857), namely Abū 'Abd Allāh al-Ḥārith b. Asad al-Muḥāsibī the ascetic Sufi master, Shāfi'ī jurist, hadith scholar and specialist of doctrine. His resting-place is in the Jumu'a mosque of al-Āṣifiyya on the eastern side of Baghdad at the top of the Shuhadā bridge. He was named al-Muḥāsibī (reckoner) because he practiced spiritual self-accounting unceasingly. He authored works on that subject and was an excellent influence on many that came after him. There was friendship between him and Imam Aḥmad and it was narrated with a sound chain that when Aḥmad first heard his discourse on *taṣawwuf* he wept until he lost consciousness. When he woke up he said, "I never heard such speech on the realities before." (Al-Dhahabī acknowledged the soundness of the chain of transmission but he could not bring himself to accept that Imam Aḥmad actually said such words.) Later in life al-Muḥāsibī rebutted the Mu'tazila by using *kalām* (dialectic theology) which Aḥmad disapproved, so the latter cut off ties with him. When Muḥāsibī died his funeral prayer was attended by only four persons.

Among al-Muḥāsibī's statements: "*Taslīm* (surrendering) is firmness at the time affliction descends, without change in one's composure whether outwardly or inwardly." "Whoever corrects his *bāṭin* (inward state) through *murāqaba* (watchfulness) and *ikhlāṣ* (sincerity), Allah shall embellish his *ẓāhir* (outward state) with mujahada and the practice of following the Sunna." Asked about intelligence he replied, "It is the light of innate qualities together with experience, and it increases and strengthens with knowledge and gentle wisdom."

24. Also among the visitations of Baghdad is the grave of the Imam and jurist Shihāb al-Dīn al-Suhrawardī (539-632/1145-1235), namely Abū Ḥafṣ 'Umar b. Muḥammad b. 'Abd Allāh al-Suhrawardī al-Qurashī al-Tamīmī al-Bakrī. Al-Dhahabī said, "the Shaykh, the Imam, the model learned scholar, the ascetic, the knower, the hadith scholar, Shaykh al-Islam, the most unique of the Sufis. He was the Shaykh of Iraq in his time in the science of spiritual reality, a practicioner of spiritual mujahada, self-sacrifice, praiseworthy way of life and perfect self-respect. He held the top leadership in the education of murids, the call of creatures to Allah and the direction of spiritual wayfaring. Our Shaykh the ascetic *muḥaddith* Ḍiyā' al-Dīn 'Īsā b. Yaḥyā al-Anṣārī dressed me with the *khirqa* (patch) of *taṣawwuf* and he said, 'Shaykh Shihāb al-Dīn al-Suhrawardī dressed me with it in Mecca, [having taken it] from his paternal uncle Abū al-Najīb [see next entry].'" Ibn Khallikān in *Wafayāt al-a'yān* mentioned that he [=Abū Ḥafṣ Shihāb al-Dīn] also took [tariqa] from Shaykh 'Abd al-Qādir al-Jaylī and other shaykhs, and that he held gatherings of admonishment for years and was the shaykh of shaykhs in Baghdad. He authored *'Awārif al-ma'ārif* (Guidelines to spiritual wisdoms), which is an encyclopedia and one of the motherbooks of the Sufis.

The author of *Marāqid Baghdād* said his resting-place is in the Suhrawardī Jumu'a mosque in the vicinity of the middle gate of eastern Baghdad, namely Bāb al-Ẓafariyya in the old Wardiyya cemetery. Today his grave has a Seljuk-style dome built on top of it resembling the dome of Sayyida Zumurrud Khātūn (Sitt Zubayda) that was built the year of his death then refurbished and renovated many times.

25. Also among the visitations of Baghdad is the grave of Shaykh Aḥmad al-Ghazālī (d. 520/1126), namely Abū al-Fatḥ Majd al-Dīn

Aḥmad b. Muḥammad b. Muḥammad b. Aḥmad the brother of Ḥujjat al-Islām. Ibn al-Mulaqqin said, "He is of the major master preachers, a person of miraculous gifts and signals. He travelled the world and served the Sufis in person." He took the tariqa from Abū Bakr al-Nassāj, from Khwājā Abū al-Qāsim al-Karakānī, from Khwājā Abū ʿAlī al-Fārmadī (his brother's shaykh and their great-uncle Abū Ḥāmid Aḥmad al-Ghazālī's student in Shāfiʿī fiqh), but Khwājā Abū ʿAlī's caliph—Khwājā Yūsuf al-Hamadhānī—disapproved of him.[3] From him the Mufti of the Iraqis and the model guide of the two parties Shaykh Ḍiyāʾ al-Dīn Abū al-Najīb ʿAbd al-Qāhir b. ʿAbd Allāh b. Muḥammad b. ʿAmmūyah al-Suhrawardī al-Bakrī al-Ṣiddīqī al-Shāfiʿī (490-563/1097-1168) took tariqa. May Allah have mercy on all of them.

Abū al-Fatḥ was attracted to seclusion but he taught in the Niẓāmiyya after his brother left it for a simpler life. The author of *Marāqid Baghdād* said, "his resting-place is on the eastern side of Baghdad in the middle of the cemetery known as Maqbarat al-Ghazālī in recent times. It is not known after which Ghazalī it was thus named since Abū al-Futūḥ actually died in Qazwīn and the grave of his brother Ḥujjat al-Islām is in Ṭūs, not Baghdad." Likewise the grave of the senior Abū Ḥāmid Aḥmad al-Ghazālī is also in Ṭūs.

Abū al-Futūḥ authored books, among them *al-Dhakhīra fī ʿilm al-baṣīra* (The supply concerning the knowledge of spiritual insight); *Lubāb al-Iḥyāʾ*, an abridgment of his brother's *Iḥyāʾ ʿulūm al-dīn*; and a treatise on *samāʿ* (musical audition) entitled *Bawāriq al-almāʿ*—published in Lucknow in 1317/1899—in which he severely condemned those that disapproved of *samāʿ*. Ṣāʿid b. Fāris compiled eighty-three sessions of his preaching in two volumes. Ibn Khallikān and others cited some of his poetry and statements. Among them,

[3] Ibn al-Jawzī, *al-Muntaẓam fī tārīkh al-mulūk wal-umam* (year 520); al-Dhahabī, *al-ʿIbar fī khabar man ghabar* (ditto); Ibn al-Subkī, *Ṭabaqāt al-Shāfiʿīyya al-kubrā* (Aḥmad al-Ghazālī al-Qadīm al-Kabīr); Ibn Ḥajar, *Lisān al-mīzān* (Aḥmad b. Muḥammad Abū al-Futūḥ al-Ṭūsī).

"Whoever suffered harm and loss in Allah, it ever rests on Allah to restore it for him." "The Sufis slept from overwhelming fatigue but your sleep is heedlessness on top of heedlessness. As long as they lived they kept watchful of Him, and when they slep He kept watch over them."

26. Also among the visitations of Baghdad is the grave of Ḥabīb al-ʿAjamī (d. 140/757), namely Abū Muḥammad Ḥabīb b. ʿĪsā b. Muḥammad al-Fārisī al-Baṣrī. He was an ascetic worshipper whose supplications were answered and whose habitual state was *qabḍ* (straitening). He narrated from al-Ḥasan al-Baṣrī, Ibn Sīrīn, Bakr b. ʿAbd Allāh al-Muzanī and Abū Tamīma Ṭurayf al-Hujaymī. From him narrated the Basrans Ḥammād b. Salama, Yazīd b. Yazīd al-Khathʿamī, Ḥammād b. ʿAṭiyya, Abū ʿAwāna, Ṣāliḥ al-Murrī, Jaʿfar b. Sulaymān al-Ḍubaʿī, Kathīr b. Yasār al-Ṭufāwī, Muʿtamir b. Sulaymān, ʿUthmān b. al-Haytham and others. He is mentioned in al-Bukhārī's biographical encyclopedia *al-Tārīkh al-kabīr*, Ḥakīm al-Tirmidhī's *Adab al-nafs* (Discipline of the ego), Abū Ṭālib al-Makkī's *Qūt al-qulūb* (Nourishment of hearts), Lālakāʾī's *Karāmāt al-awliyāʾ* and others. Ibn ʿAbd al-Barr mentioned that "he was trustworthy and above trustworthy, but he narrated little." From him narrated Ḥammād b. Salama, Abū ʿAwāna, Jaʿfar b. Sulaymān, Dāwūd al-Ṭāʾī, Muʿtamir b. Sulaymān and others. His wife ʿAmra was of the righteous women whom Ibn al-Jawzī mentioned in *Ṣifat al-ṣafwa.* His resting-place is in the mosque named after him on the western side of Baghdad north of the Shuhadāʾ bridge in the vicinity of *al-Tarbiyat al-islāmiyya* madrasa. Shaykh Yūnus al-Sāmarrāʾī said in *Marāqid Baghdād* that the correct position is he died in Basra where Ibn Baṭṭūṭa said he saw his grave, and Allah knows best.

Among the statements reported from Ḥabīb al-ʿAjamī: "I fear that Allah will say to me, 'Ḥabīb, show me one *tasbīḥ* by which you glorified Me in 60 years in which the devil did not have any part at all.' What shall I say? There is no way out. I shall say, 'My nurturing Lord, it is as You say. I have come to you with my hands shackled to my neck!'" Ibn al-Mulaqqin said, "And this is a man who had worshipped Allah for sixty years, a man engrossed in Him, who never pursued anything from the world at all—then how will we fare?" The chain of transmission of the Sufi patch is related from him, from al-Ḥasan al-Baṣrī, from ʿAlī b. Abī Ṭālib–Allah be well-pleased with him. It moves down from him to Dāwūd al-Ṭā'ī, to Maʿrūf al-Karkhī.

Ḥabīb was in fact a merchant and had a share of worldly possessions but al-Ḥasan's exhortation fell into his heart, after which he gave alms of 40,000 and made do with little, worshipping Allah until he died. He would be seen in Basra on the day of *tarwiya* (watering the pilgrims =8 Dhūl-Ḥijja) and he would be seen in ʿArafa the very next day. It was mentioned by Ibn ʿAsākir in his *Tārīkh* and al-Dhahabī in *Tārīkh al-Islām*.

X
Continuation on the etiquette of visiting the graves; more reference-works in addition to what was already cited

Shaykh ʿAbd al-Qādir was related to say in the *Ghunya*: "It is disliked to walk in the cemetery with shoes on. It is desirable for whoever enters it to say, 'O Allah, the nurturing Lord of these decomposed bodies and hollowed-out bones that have exited the abode of the world in a state of belief in You, bless Muḥammad and the Family of Muḥammad and cause to descend upon them a spirit from You and salam from me.' Then one says, '*As-salāmu ʿalaykum*, abode of a believing people, and we, if Allah wills, shall verily be joining you.' But when one visits a grave one must not place his hand on it nor must one kiss it, for it is the habit of the Jews. Nor does one sit on it, nor does one lean on it, nor does one tread on top of it except if there is no other way. Then let one recite eleven times the 112th Sura and other Suras of the Qurʾān, gifting the reward of that to the dweler of the grave by saying, 'O Allah, if You have rewarded me for reciting this Sura, then I have donated its reward to the dweller of this grave.' Then one asks one's need of Allah."

What is meant in the above expression "when one visits a grave one must not place his hand on it nor must one kiss it" is the worldly way, not touching it or kissing it in the sense of seeking the hereafter. The statement of the Shāfiʿī imam Khayr al-Dīn al-Ramlī was already mentioned that "as for kissing the tombs of the friends of Allah and their thresholds, there is no disagreement as to its permissibility. More than that, there is no dislike in kissing their thresholds for the sake of blessing." More than that, there is no dislike according to Imam Aḥmad at all as is well-known. His son ʿAbd Allāh related it from him as narrated by al-Dhahabī in his *Tārīkh al-Islām*, his *Siyar aʿlām al-nubalāʾ* and his *Muʿjam al-shuyūkh* as we documented it in *Tuḥfat al-labīb fīl-masāʾil al-ṣūfiyya* (The gift to the enlightened on Sufi issues) among many other evidentiary proofs.

Furthermore, the dislike concerns common graves. As for visiting the righteous in their graves then one stands before them exactly as if they were present in their worldly life, i.e. without circumambulating them and without rubbing them. One lowers one's voice and guards one's thoughts and one's gaze, not speaking before them about any worldly matter but rather greeting them with calm, respect and dignity. Then one recites whatever Allah wills of the noble Qur'ān and blessings on the Prophet–upon him the blessings and peace of Allah–followed by the donation of its reward to him and to the dweller in the grave and those with a right to it. If the place is wide enough one may pray two cycles of prayer, taking care to avoid facing the grave. Then one supplicates for them and for himself.

Supplication is required from the beginning to the end of the visitation—perhaps it is a place and a time whereby supplication is answered. I have heard verbatim and witnessed the practice of the Shaykhs of the most distinguished Naqshbandi Tariqa to the effect that the spiritual presences of the Elect Prophet–upon him the blessings and peace of Allah–amd of his noble Family and Companions and the Prophets–upon them peace–and the spiritual Poles of the Chain are present at the grave-station of every wali that is visited. So what is best for the visitor is to intend the visit to the Prophet and greet him first upon witnessing the grave-station, then the Family, then the Companions, then the Prophets, then his Shaykhs, then the dweller of the grave. He should not omit to renew his witnessing of the faith three times in front of this wali and ask forgiveness seventy times before reciting the Qur'ān then, after reciting, he entrusts the reward of what he recited with the Messenger of Allah–upon him the blessings and peace of Allah–and with the dweller of the grave until the Day of Resurrection. To that intention does he recite the Fatiha and the last three Suras. Our Master Shaykh Muṣṭafā b. al-Sayyid Ibrāhīm Baṣīr al-Ḥasanī al-Maghribī al-Darqāwī–Allah have mercy on them–would never omit the recitation of the Sura of Yā Sīn nor would our Naqshbandi Shaykhs.

Likewise I saw Shaykh al-Jaylī recite the 112th Sura (Ikhlāṣ) eleven times just as they did and as instructed in the *Ghunya*, per what is narrated from our liege lord ʿAlī–Allah be well-pleased with him–from the Prophet–upon him the blessings and peace of Allah: "**Whoever passes by the graves and recites *Qul huwa-l-Lāhu aḥad* eleven times then donates its reward to the dead shall be given of reward to the number of the dead.**"

مَنْ مَرَّ عَلَى الْمَقَابِرِ وَقَرَأَ قُلْ هُوَ اللهُ أَحَدٌ إِحْدَى عَشْرَةَ مَرَّةً ثُمَّ وَهَبَ أَجْرَهُ لِلْأَمْوَاتِ أُعْطِيَ مِنَ الْأَجْرِ بِعَدَدِ الْأَمْوَاتِ

It was cited by the Hadith master Ibn Surūr al-Maqdisī in *Juzʾ wuṣūl al-qirāʾati lil-mayyit* (monograph on the recitation reaching the dead) and he sourced it to al-Dāraquṭnī, the Qadi Abū Yaʿlā and the *Musnad* of Abū Bakr al-Najjād. Daylamī related it in *Musnad al-firdaws*, Ghulām al-Khallāl in *Faḍl Sūrat al-Ikhlāṣ* and Rāfiʿī in *Tārīkh Qazwīn*. Abū Bakr al-Khallāl also narrated in his monograph on recitation over the graves that Ḥasan b. al-Haytham told him, "Khaṭṭāb would come to me with his hand counting numbers and he would say, 'When you reach the graves then recite *Qul huwa-l-Lāhu aḥad* and give its reward to the dwellers of the graves.'" He also narrated therein from al-Shaʿbī that he said, "When one of the *Anṣār* died they would visit his grave and read the Qurʾān there." Al-Thaʿlabī narrates in his *Tafsīr* with a weak chain because of Ayyūb b. Mudrik al-Ḥanafī from Anas that the Prophet–upon him the blessings and peace of Allah–said, "**Whoever enters the graveyard and recites the Sura of Yāsīn, Allah lightens for them and gives him good deeds to the number of its dwellers.**"

مَنْ دَخَلَ الْمَقَابِرَ فَقَرَأَ سُورَةَ يٰس خَفَّفَ اللهُ عَنْهُمْ وَكَانَ لَهُ بِعَدَدِ مَنْ فِيهَا حَسَنَاتٌ

Qurṭubī cites it in his *Tafsīr* and *Tadhkira* as does Ibn Surūr in *Juzʾ wuṣūl al-qirāʾati lil-mayyit*.

Also among the reference-works on this issue which we have is al-Hakkārī's (d. 486/1093) *Hadiyyat al-aḥyā' lil-amwāt wa-mā yaṣilu ilayhim min al-naf'i wal-thawāb 'alā mamarri al-awqāt* (The gift of the living to the dead and what reaches them of benefit and reward time after time); Sarūjī's (d. 710/1310) *Nafaḥāt al-nasamāt fī wuṣūl ihdā' al-thawāb lil-amwāt* (The wafts of breezes on the arrival of reward to the dead); Ibn Ḥajar's *al-Qawl bil-iḥsān al-'amīm fī intifā' al-mayyit bil-Qur'ān al-aẓīm* (The position that there is universal excellence in the benefitting of the dead from the magnificent Qur'ān); Sakhāwī's *Qurrat al-'ayn bil-masarrat al-ḥāṣila lil-thawāb lil-mayyit wal-abawayn* (The coolness of the eye with the gladness that ensues from the reward to the dead and the parents) and his *al-Īḍāḥ wal-tabyīn bi-mas'alat al-talqīn* (Clarification and exposition of the issue of dictation over graves); Shawkānī's *Luḥūq thawāb al-qirā'at al-muhdāt min al-aḥyā' ilā al-amwāt* (Following up of the reward of recitation that is donated by the living to the dead); Sayyid Muḥammad b. Aḥmad b. 'Abd al-Bārī al-Ahdal's (1241-1298/1826-1881) *Ifādat al-ṭullāb bi-aḥkām al-qirā'a 'alā al-mawtā wa-wuṣūl al-thawāb* (Apprising the students of the rulings of recitation over the dead and the reaching of reward) which we read in full in 2008 with Ḥabīb 'Alī b. Muḥammad b. Muḥsin al-Ḥāmid Bakrī al-Tarīmī in Brunei; Sayyid Muḥammad al-'Arabī al-Tabbānī's *Is'āf al-muslimīn wal-muslimāt bi-jawāz al-qirā'ati wa-wuṣūli thawābihā ilā al-amwāt* (Assistance of Muslim men and women concerning the permissibility of recitation and the reaching of its reward to the dead); and Sayyid Muḥammad b. 'Alawī al-Mālikī's *Taḥqīq al-āmāl fī-mā yanfa'u al-mayyita min al-a'māl* (Realization of hopes concerning what benefits the dead of works.

Shaykh 'Abd al-Qādir said in the *Ghunya*: "When he finishes"—i.e. supplicating—"he wipes his face with his hands." This practice is firmly-established as authentic in transmission both from the Prophet–upon him the blessings and peace of Allah–and from the Companions–Allah be well-pleased with them as well as from the subsequent generation-layers of the righteous predecessors. Likewise the raising of the hands in supplication and the reciting of the supplication aloud together with those present saying *āmīn*.

When he wants to leave he gives salam and exits quietly. The shaykhs disliked for one to leave backwards (without turning one's back to the grave) because the Companions did not do that with the Prophet–upon him the blessings and peace of Allah and may He be well-pleased with them. But if one turns around and leaves the *maqām* then turns back as if giving a last farewell look full of longing it is enough, and Allah knows best. Let one "not show enmity in *du'ā*" (Hadith) i.e. one should not specifically exclude or exclusively request, or show bad manners or go overboard in loudness or make oneself shout to make everyone around him hear.

We saw in the court of the Jaylānī grave the spectacular sight of beardless followers of the Kasnazāniyya Tariqa with extremely long hair dancing and shaking their heads to the sound of massive drums. The Shaykh said in the *Gunya*, "Mosques have been instituted for the remembrance of Allah Most High and prayer, so they should be kept free and clear of all that is other than that." Then he said, "Section on sounds: sounds that come from the recitation of poetry that has nothing to do with taverns or instruments are two types: indifferent and forbidden. The indifferent is that which entails no frivolity while the forbidden is what entails frivolity. As for what is produced in the context of taverns or musical instruments then it is forbidden regardless whether it is devoid of frivolity or accompanied with it. The only difference is that when any frivolity accompanies there are two reasons for its being forbidden." May Allah grant mercy to whoever preserves his *maqām* from such, and from the striking of the large bell that rings every hour at the door of the mosque—an ugly contravention of the Sunna since it is mentioned in Abū Dāwūd from 'Umar–Allah be well-pleased with him–that the Prophet–upon him the blessings and peace of Allah–said, "**Verily there is with every bell a devil,**" especially in light of the fact that it resembles the chime of a church bell.

إِنَّ مَعَ كلِّ جَرَسٍ شَيْطَاناً

Would also that the overseers of the Shaykh's *ḥawl* (yearly celebration) set aside an hour for the hearing of some of his wisdoms and advices the way it was in his time, if only in imitation of the past! And if they did, it would be beneficiary for all and full of blessing. As for the loud statement of *lā ilāha illā-Lāh* followed by the recitation of the last two Suras by the congregation in the Shaykh's mosque right after *iqāma* and before the opening *takbīr*, it ought not to cause one to abandon the well-known Sunna supplications that are appropriate to that moment—whether individual or congregational—because it is a time when supplication is answered as the Prophet–upon him the blessings and peace of Allah–informed of it, such as the *wasīla* supplication which also signifies collectedness and high manners in the presence of Allah.

We conclude with Qārī's advice in his commentary on *al-Ḥiṣn al-ḥaṣīn* (The impregnable fortress), a volume of supplications and *dhikr* which the Imam and arch-expert of the Qur'ān Ibn al-Jazarī al-Dimashqī–Allah have mercy on them–wrote at the time Damascus was surrounded by the Mongols and Crusaders: "When you visit the grave of a Prophet or a wali or a learned scholar or anyone besides them and you are in some terrible affliction and you want for the soul of the dweller of that grave to be present for you to voice your complaint to him—i.e. with the tongue of your state or of your speech—so that he will intercede for you in the presence of the All-Sovereign of all in order that He will suffice you against what has troubled you and cure you of your ailment, recite *Qul huwa-l-Lāhu aḥad* ten times (and if you precede it with the Heart of the Qur'ān—I mean the Sura of Yāsīn—it will be better and faster [in response]), the two refuge-grantors [=Sura 113 and 114] three times each, the Opening of the Book, and the Beautiful Names after the beginning and the end of the Sura of al-Baqara. Close your eyes and collect all of your heart then say, *lā ilāha illā-l-Lāh* three times, *ALLĀH* three times with elongation of the *Ā*. Then pause and say, *assalāmu 'alaykum wa-raḥmatu-l-Lāhi wa-barakātuh yā Sayyidī* [name], or *yā Shaykh*, or *yā Ustādhī*, or *yā Rasūla-l-Lāh*. And you expose what has befallen you of troubles to the one you are visiting: the All-Coverer of faults shall dispel them by the intercession of the dweller of the visitation. And this is among the greatest of benefits." This is from Mullā 'Alī al-Qārī's commentary on *al-Ḥiṣan al-ḥaṣīn* as cited by Shaykh Yūsuf al-Nabhānī in *Shawāhid al-ḥaqq*, quoting Imam Muṣṭafā al-Bakrī al-Khalwatī (1099-1162/1688-1749)—the student of Shaykh 'Abd al-Ghanī al-Nābulusī—who was citing al-Qārī.

The shahid and Mufti of Lebanon Shaykh Hasan Khalid (1921-1989) related from his teacher the Mufti of Syria Shaykh Abū al-Yusr 'Ābidīn that he would tell them to supplicate at the grave of Shaykh al-Islam the Quṭb Imam al-Nawawī–Allah have mercy on all of them–because supplication is answered there. May Allah grant mercy to the seekers of intermediary and to the intermediaries and may He benefit us and all Muslims with them except whoever refuses. Muwaffaq al-Dīn b. 'Abd al-Raḥmān b. Makkī b. 'Uthmān al-Shāri'ī al-Shāfi'ī al-Anṣārī (d. 615/1218) described in *Murshid al-zuwwār ilā qubūr al-abrār* (The trusted guide of visitors to the graves of the virtuous) twenty tasks in fulfillment of the etiquette of the visitation to the graves of the righteous including sincerity of intention, designating the day of Jumu'a or the fourth day of the week [=Wednesday], preferably seeking the graves of the Prophets, the Prophetic family, the Companions and one's relatives—spiritual and biological—together with the recitation of the Qur'ān, the invocation of blessings on the Prophet–upon him the blessings and peace of Allah, supplication for oneself, the mention of the virtues of the one being visited at his grave, and other than that. Success is all from Allah.

XI
Proprieties of outer and inner travel, dispensation and strictness

"The nobler of the two journeys is *al-safar al-bāṭin* (the inner journey)" (Ghazālī, *Iḥyā'*).

Shaykh 'Abd al-Qādir said in the *Ghunya*: "Section on the high manners of travel and companionship therein. When one wants to travel let him pray two cycles of prayer then say, 'O Allah, grant the reach of a reaching of goodness and forgiveness from You and good pleasure! In Your hand is all goodness and You are, over all things, All-Powerful. O Allah, You are the companion in travel and the successor in the spouse and the property and the child. O Allah, make easy for us the journey and fold up for us the distance. O Allah, verily I seek refuge in you from the fatigue of travel and a sorrowful return and an evil appearance in the spouse and the property and the child.' Once he has settled on his mount he says, *glorified is the One Who has subjected this to us when we were never its matches, and verily we are, unto our nurturing Lord, indeed turning back!* (al-Zukhruf 43:13-14).

﴿ سُبْحَٰنَ ٱلَّذِى سَخَّرَ لَنَا هَٰذَا وَمَا كُنَّا لَهُۥ مُقْرِنِينَ ﴿١٣﴾ وَإِنَّآ إِلَىٰ رَبِّنَا لَمُنقَلِبُونَ ﴿١٤﴾ ﴾ الزخرف ١٣-١٤.

"When he returns from travel he prays two cycles of prayer and says, 'Returning, repenting, worshipping our nurturing Lord, prainsing and giving thanks.' He must keep quiet and keep excellent companionship with abundant beneficialness to his brethren. Let him strictly avoid gossip. **He must come out of his blameworthy attributes onto his praiseworthy attributes. So he comes out of his whim onto the pursuit of His protecting Friend's good pleasure by rectifying his Godfearingness**. He ought to interact with his companions, throughout his journey, with excellent character, beautiful humor and avoidance of disagreement and argument in all things. Let him busy himself with serving his travel companions and not use anyone's service except in necessity. **Let one always strive to be in a state of ritual purity during his journey**.

"Also of the proprieties of companionship is that one should stop and stand with one's companion when the latter is stranded; give him water when he is thirsty; be gentle with him when he is exasperated; humor him when he is angry; guard him and his saddle-pack when he sleeps; give him priority when the provision is scarce; share with him any good fortune without keeping it to himself; neither keep a secret from him nor divulge his secret; not ask his help except in the best manner; rebutting any slander of him (or of his); mentioning him in the best way among the fellow-travellers neither putting him to shame nor complaining about him to them; bearing with his harm; counseling him when he consults him; asking him about his name, his country and his lineage even if he is above him in station; impressing upon the fellow-travellers that he is his follower even if the reverse is true in reality; showing his follower his defects in the way of faithful advice, not in that of rebuke and chiding.

"One must seek refuge in Allah from everything he fears whenever he moves to a place or alights at some stop or sits in some spot or sleeps there, by saying: 'I seek refuge in Allah and in the complete words of Allah that no virtuous one and no sinner can trespass, and in the beautiful Names of Allah in their entirety, the ones I know and the ones I do not know, against the evil of what He created and dispersed and brought into being, and against the evil of what comes down from the sky and what ascends therein, and against the evil of what grows in the earth and what comes out of it, and against the strifes of the night and the day, and against every knocker at the door other than for goodness, O All-Merciful!'

أَعُوذُ بِاللهِ وَبِكَلِمَاتِ اللهِ التَّامَّاتِ الَّتِي لَا يُجَاوِزُهُنَّ بَرٌّ وَلَا فَاجِرٌ، وَبِأَسْمَاءِ اللهِ الْحُسْنَى كُلِّهَا مَا عَلِمْتُ مِنْهَا وَمَا لَمْ أَعْلَمْ، مِنْ شَرِّ مَا خَلَقَ وَذَرَأَ وَبَرَأَ، وَمِنْ شَرِّ مَا يَنْزِلُ مِنَ السَّمَاءِ وَمَا يَعْرُجُ فِيهَا، وَمِنْ شَرِّ مَا ذَرَأَ فِي الْأَرْضِ وَمَا يَخْرُجُ مِنْهَا، وَمِنْ فِتَنِ اللَّيْلِ وَالنَّهَارِ، وَمِنْ كُلِّ طَارِقٍ إِلَّا طَارِقًا يَطْرُقُ بِخَيْرٍ يَا رَحْمٰنُ

"It is also desirable for the traveller to carry a stick and strive never to be without it, in light of what Maymūn b. Mahrān narrated from Ibn ʿAbbās–Allah be well-pleased with him and his father–who said, 'Carrying a stick is the Sunna of the Prophets and the mark of the believers.' And it is permissible to kill any animal that might harm."

All of the above concerns the general public. As for the special ones, Shaykh ʿAbd al-Qādir said in a different part of his book: "When the *faqīr* wants to travel from his country the first thing he must do is to make peace with his adversaries and ask permission of his parents or whoever has their status in respect of duties and rights over him such as uncles on both sides and grandparents. Once they agree to that he departs. If he has dependants who will be harmed and put into straitened circumstances by his trip then such a trip will not be wholeseome for him until he first takes care of their welfare, or unless he takes them with him. The Prophet–upon him the blessings and peace of Allah–said, '**It is a grave enough sin for someone to desert those whom he provides for**' [narrated from ʿAbd Allāh b. ʿAmr b. al-ʿĀṣ by Aḥmad, Abū Dāwūd, al-Nasāʾī in *al-Sunan al-kubrā*, Ibn Ḥibbān, Ḥākim and Abū Nuʿaym in the *Ḥilya*.]

كَفَى بِالْمَرْءِ إِثْمًا أَنْ يُضَيِّعَ مَنْ يَقُوتُ

"It is also a precondition for the *faqīr*, when he travels, that his heart must be with him. It must neither be turning around to some attachment he left behind nor attached to some pursuit ahead of him. Wherever he alights his heart must be with him and his heart must be free of all things. He ought not to fall short in his spiritual devotions that he normally did at home. **For travel for them is an increase in their spiritual states, so there ought not to be a gap in his deeds and his states during his travel.** Dispensations are only for the weak and the common public—and what will the strong and the elite do with dispensations? Rather strict resolve is forever their lot in all of their states, the enablement for success is enfolding them, mercy is descending on them, the guard is standing with them, protection is permanent for them, the Beloved is sitting with them and *uns* (intimacy) with Him keeps increasing, sufficiency upholds them, spiritual supplies are successive and uninterrupted, the divine gaze never leaves them and their armies are swarming constantly in the fray for them. So travel is stronger for them and more lenient and beautiful for what their immediate concerns, for therein is remoteness from the despotic avenues of livelihood and people that are the very idols—more replete with misguidance than crosses and harsher than Satan."

The high manners of Mawlana Shaykh Nazim in travel

To Allah belongs the abundant good that flowed from our Master Mawlana Shaykh Nazim–Allah sanctify his secret–for he never neglected the eight *rak'ats* of the Ḍuḥā prayer or the six post-Maghrib voluntary *rak'as* or the *tahajjud* prayer whether at home or abroad, and he would instruct for of all that to be observed even if he were at the airport or the hotel in some eastern or western country. He practiced the way of *'azīma* (strict observance) according to the school of Imam al-Shāfi'ī whereby he would not shorten prayers, he would recite the *basmala* aloud, he would recite both the *qunūṭ*s of the dawn and the *witr* prayers, he would pray each prayer with all of its *sunan* and meritorious acts as well as all its devotions before and after the obligatory prayer and in congregation, together with calling people to submission, lavishing heavenly advice on the old and the young, the simple and the educated, wearing the turban and the mantle with free-flowing beards, wearing the sunna ring, carrying the staff, keeping ritual purity at home and abroad, shining a constant elevated disposition on all, feeding people, sleeping little and keeping all the Sunnas and the devotions of Tariqa.

I noticed from some fellow travellers to Iraq one or more that might sing and bang the drum from the start to the end of the time for prayer without praying—per the dispensation—while chanting, "the heart trembles and the eye weeps at the remembrance of Allah."

القلبُ يَخشَع والعينُ تَدمَع بذكر الله

Then he will sleep the night and not get up for the dawn prayer until after its time. Then, in the day, he will sway again to the sound of spiritual poetry and say, "nights of linkage! If they were sold I would buy them with my soul! But they are neither sold nor bought."

ليالِ وِصالٍ لو تُباعُ شَرَيتُها بِروحي ولكنْ لا تُباعُ وَلا تُشرَى

Shah Naqshband–Allah sanctify his secret–said, "Whoever speaks about stations and states he did not acquire, will be deprived of them." I asked about it Sayyidī al-Shaykh Muṣṭafā Baṣīr–Allah have mercy on him–and he replied with forgiveness, "Let him sing what the righteous said and form the intention to reach their station that made them say what they said."

Shaykh ʿAbd al-Qādir further said, "When renown and acceptance take place for a *faqīr* in some place he ought to leave it at once and confound that acceptance in his own mind so that he will not be banished from the presence of Allah and be veiled from Him, lest his only lot should be creatures. This is only in case whim and proclivity are still there. If they have passed away then there is no existence for creatures and their acceptance has no effect. They are outside the heart and between the two there are guards protecting the heart from the intrusion of creatures lest *shirk* (polytheism) ensues and pure monotheism becomes unravelled."

The faqih of the Tāza valley in northern Morocco, Muḥammad b. Muḥammad b. Manṣūr al-ʿĀmirī al-Talamsānī (d. circa 1195/ 1781) opened his poem describing his journey from Tāza to the two Holy Sanctuaries and back through Syro-Palestine with the lines:

أَزْمِعِ السَّيْرَ إِنْ دَهَـــــتْ أَدْوَاءُ * إِلَى شَفِيـــعِ الْأَنَامِ فَهْوَ الدَّوَاءُ

وَادَّخِرْ عَوْلَةَ الْعِيَـــالِ فَلَا تَدْرِي * بِأَيِّ الْأُمُورِ يَأْتِي الْقَضَـــــاءُ

وَاسْتَحِلِ الْإِخْوَانَ وَالْأَهْلَ مِمَّـــا * كَانَ مِنْكَ وَإِنْ يَكُونُوا أَسَاؤُوا

Journey with resolve if ailments have no cure
to the intercesssor of all, for he is the remedy.
And store up the dependants' store—you know not
in what circumstances comes the decree.
And get a pardon from brethren and kin for
what transpired from you even if they did harm.

The weak servant has striven to furnish the family before every journey taken together with submission to the decree of my nurturing Lord, reliance upon him, and following the example of His caliphs in the Sunna of His Prophet–upon him and his Family, Companions and inheritors the blessings and peace of Allah.

XII
Keeping assiduous company with the righteous, study and attachment with a perfect Shaykh

The upshot of this discourse is that the Shaykhs are in agreement over the necessity of keeping assiduous company with the righteous for the seeker of deliverance from the part of the ego and its evils and for the realization of the divine command, *O you who believe! Beware the One God and be with the truthful ones* (al-Tawba 9:119),

﴿ يَٰٓأَيُّهَا ٱلَّذِينَ ءَامَنُوا۟ ٱتَّقُوا۟ ٱللَّهَ وَكُونُوا۟ مَعَ ٱلصَّٰدِقِينَ ﴿١١٩﴾ ﴾ التوبة

and the Prophetic supplication that was authentically transmitted, "**O Allah! Do not leave me to my *nafs* for the blink of an eye**" [narrated from Abū Bakrat al-Thaqafī, Anas, Abū Hurayra, Jābir, Ibn ʿUmar and, in *mursal* mode, ʿUbayd b. ʿUmayr and Qatāda by al-Ṭayālisī; Ibn Abī Shayba; Aḥmad; al-Bukhārī (*Adab al-mufrad*); Abū Dāwūd; al-Nasāʾī; al-Ṭabarānī; al-Bazzār; Nasāʾī; Kharāʾiṭī; Ṭabarānī; Abū Bakr al-Shāfiʿī (*Ghaylāniyyāt*); al-Ṭabarānī; al-Khaṭīb; al-Dāraquṭnī; al-Ṭabarī; al-Wāḥidī (*Basīṭ*); al-Ḍiyāʾ in the *Mukhtāra* and Ibn Ḥajar in *Natāʾij al-afkār* both rated it *ḥasan*].

اللهمَّ لا تَكِلْنِي إلى نَفْسِي طَرْفَةَ عَيْنٍ

The means for implementing that necessity is to travel to them and serve them and be present with them body and soul in their presence and in their absence, which is the secret of the noble *rābiṭa* (firm connection). The latter connection can only be with with a perfect shaykh who masters learning and is a spiritual knower of the way stations of the wayfarers on the way to the King of kings, and fully cognizant of the minutiae of spiritual direction and wayfaring as clarified by the Imam of the Tariqa and the arch-helper of creatures Shāh Bahāʾ al-Dīn Naqshband. One must not suffice oneself with someone lesser in realization except until he will eventually lead him to the perfect shaykh. One must make sure to avoid deniers and enviers because sitting with them causes darkness to descend on the heart and veils one from the truth—Allah grant refuge! One must firmly intend to keep company with the sincere ones and the truthful ones in the Tariqa, giving each their due station, so he gives respect to the advanced one and prizes him so that he will not be deprived of his knowledge and the blessing of his seniority as an authorized deputy of the Shaykh. For the newcomer is not like the one whose hair has grayed at the thresholds of the Awliya even if it is true that "The path belongs to him who is truthful, not to him who came first" as stated by the Qādirī master Shaykh Ḥāzim Nāyif Abū Ghazālah al-Ḥusaynī in *al-Ajwibat al-ghazāliyya ʿalā al-asʾilat al-ṣūfiyya* (The Ghazālah answers to the Sufi questions).

الطَّرِيقُ لِمَنْ صَدَقَ لَا لِمَنْ سَبَقَ

Most importantly, murids pay special attention to those that have served Mawlana Shaykh Hisham from the first hour without becoming turncoats, and to those concerning whom he would use special phrases, for example, "So and so is like ten murids" or "When so and so speaks it is as if I am speaking" and other such expressions.

One should also beware of the possessors of *aḥwāl* (states) and *talwīn* (variegation) among shaykhs not to mention murids, for they do not know what they say. Mawlana Shaykh Nazim said to us, "**The possessor of states, even mountains find him unbearable;**"

صَاحِبُ الأَحْوَالِ لَا تَتَحَمَّلُهُ الْجِبَالُ

and he said in Lefke to the writer of these lines, "**Shaykh so and so has more *ʿilm*** (knowledge) **and Shaykh Hisham has more *tamkīn*** (stability)." See further up the example Sayyid Rifāʿī gave for *tamkīn*.

الشيخ فُلان أَكْثَرُ عِلْماً والشيخ هِشَام أَكْثَرُ تَمْكِيناً

Furthermore, the obtainment of outward knowledge has priority over that of inward knowledge since the latter is impossible without the former as clearly stated by Imam Mālik. Qadi ʿIyāḍ narrated in *Tartīb al-masālik* that someone asked Mālik about something related to *ʿilm al-bāṭin* (inward knowledge), whereupon he became angry and said, "**None has knowledge of *ʿilm al-bāṭin* except he who has knowledge of *ʿilm al-ẓāhir*; once he fully knows *ʿilm al-ẓāhir* and has put it into practice, Allah opens for him *ʿilm al-bāṭin*.**"

عِلْمُ البَاطِنِ لَا يَعْرِفُهُ إِلَّا مَنْ عَرَفَ عِلْمَ الظَّاهِرِ؛ فَمَتَى عَرَفَ عِلْمَ الظَّاهِرِ وَعَمِلَ بِهِ: فَتَحَ اللهُ عَلَيْهِ عِلْمَ الْبَاطِنِ

This is why they have advised that the wayfarer must first obtain outward knowledge before mixing with the Sufis because when he mixes with them before learning it, their states will enrapture him and it will become difficult for him to learn. He might even turn into an enemy of knowledge and its people, thinking that spiritual realities and gnoses can only be taken from spiritual intuitions, dreams and states. So he will neglect legal rulings and wash his hands of any study or book learning, considering it a shameful defect, ignoring the Prophet's–upon him blessings and peace of Allah–mass-transmitted instruction, "**The pursuit of knowledge is a categorical obligation for every Muslim,**"

طَلَبُ الْعِلْمِ فَرِيضَةٌ عَلَى كُلِّ مُسْلِمٍ

and the recommendation of our liege lord ʿUmar–Allah be well-pleased with him–saying, *tafaqqahū qabla an tusawwadū*, "**Acquire knowledge before you are given leadership**" in Bukhārī and others—and the highest of all is the spiritual leadership.

تَفَقَّهُوا قَبْلَ أَنْ تُسَوَّدُوا

Allah Most High knows best. He said, *We raise in levels whomever We wish; and above every possessor of knowledge there is one with vaster knowledge* (Yūsuf 12:76),

﴿ نَرْفَعُ دَرَجَٰتٍ مَّن نَّشَآءُ ۗ وَفَوْقَ كُلِّ ذِى عِلْمٍ عَلِيمٌ ﴾ يوسف

and the head of the matter is fear of the nurturing Lord and pure hope in Him with brokenness of spirit. Allah also said, *and the one that came bringing the pure truth and confirmed it as true, those ones—they are those that guard themselves* (al-Zumar 39:33).

﴿ وَٱلَّذِى جَآءَ بِٱلصِّدْقِ وَصَدَّقَ بِهِۦٓ ۙ أُو۟لَٰٓئِكَ هُمُ ٱلْمُتَّقُونَ ﴿٣٣﴾ ﴾ الزمر

O Allah! Grant our souls their Godfearingness and purify them. You are the best of those that purify them. You are their protecting friend and their master. And may Allah bless and greet our liege lord Muḥammad and his Family and Companions abundantly.

Index of Quranic Verses

al-Baqara
2:154 ... 31, 33
2:281 ... 87

Āl 'Imrān
3:169 ... 31, 32

al-A'rāf
7:201 ... 53

Barā'a/al-Tawba
9:119 ... 13, 119

Yūnus–upon him peace–
10:62 ... 17, 18

Yūsuf–upon him peace–
12:76 ... 122

al-Kahf
18:18 ... 69
18:62 ... 58
18:66 ... 65
18:78 ... 66

al-Nūr
24:30 ... 94

al-Naml
27:88 ... 33

al-'Ankabūt
29:1-2 ... 52

al-Aḥzāb
33:23 ... 13

al-Malā'ika/Fāṭir
35:10 ... 73

al-Zumar
39:33 ... 122

al-Mu'min/Ghāfir
40:3 ... 24
40:46 ... 43

al-Zukhruf
43:13-14 ... 113

al-Dhāriyāt
51:56 ... 14

al-Raḥmān
55:22 ... 73
55:46 ... 54
59:10 ... 70

al-Burūj
85:4 ... 32

al-Fajr
89:2 ... 88

al-Ikhlāṣ
112:1-4 ... 107

Index of Hadiths

Acquire knowledge before you are given leadership, 121
Allah! [Beware] Allah with respect to your brethren in the graves!, 45
Allah has servants who are neither Prophets nor martyrs but whom they yearn to resemble, 18
As for my cheerfulness it was for what I saw of the honorable status of his soul, 51
Awliyā are on pulpits of light, 15
Blessed are the strangers!, 19
Breaking the bone of the dead is like breaking his bone when alive, 42
Do not shame your deceased ones with the bad deeds that you do, 45
Fātiḥa is the best Sura in the Qur'ān and a cure for every ailment, 85
How are you this morning O Ḥāritha?, 23
I am according to My servant's thought about Me, 59
I bear witness these are shahids in the presence of Allah, 51
I had forbidden you from visiting the graves. Now do visit them, 56
I had forbidden you three things and am now commanding you to do them, 56
I passed by Mūsā on the night I was taken on a night journey, 30
I recognized Ja'far among some angel companions of his, 42
I swear all of you are not hearing what I say any better than they, 39
It is a grave enough sin for someone to desert those he provides for, 115
Let each one's budget be the same as the traveller's provision, 84
Make beautiful the shrouds of your deceased ones, 41
My love is for those that love one another for My sake, 16, 17
No man visits his brother's grave and sits besides it but the latter welcomes his company, 40
None of you greets them to the Day of Resurrection but they definitely answer him, 51
None passes by his brother believer's grave whom he knew in life, 41
O Abū Jahl b. Hishām! O Umayya b. Khalaf! O 'Utba b. Rabī'a! O Shayba b. Rabī'a!, 39

O Allah! Do not leave me to my *nafs* for the blink of an eye, 119
O Bilal! Do not feel penury from the Owner of the Throne, 99
On the Day of Resurrection Allāh seats them on pedestals of light, 18
One's best earning is the work of one's right hand, 94
People will come to Allah on the Day of Resurrection, their light like that of the sun, 19
People! Listen to this, understand it, and know it, 18
Person follows the faith-system of their friend, A 21
Prophet took the pickaxe from Salmān's hand and struck the rock hard three times, The 83
Prophet visited the graves of the shahids at Uḥud, The 52
Prophets are alive in their graves, praying, The 30
Pursuit of knowledge is a categorical obligation for every Muslim, 121
Salmān is one of us, the people of the House, 82
There are, of the servants of Allah, certain servants about whom the Prophets and shahids yearn, 17
They are of the strangers from here and there, 18
Those that love one another are in the shade of His Throne, 16
Those who love one another for the majesty of Allah are on pulpits of light. Prophets and martyrs will long to be in their position, 15
Verily Allah has made it prohibited for the earth to consume the bodies ot the Prophets, 30
Verily Allah shall bring the provision of every morrow, 99
Verily the deceased is hurt in his grave by whatever would hurt him in his own house, 42
Verily the deceased recognizes whoever carries him, 45
Verily there is with every bell a devil, 109
Verily your deeds are shown to your close relatives and kindred, 44
Were it not that you would end up not burying one another I would have supplicated, 44
When a human being dies his deeds cease but for three things, 43
When a man passes by a grave that he recognizes and gives salam, 40
When they [=the *awliyā*] are seen, Allah is remembered, 14
Whoever enters the graveyard and recites the Sura of Yāsīn, 107
Whoever passes by the graves and recites *Qul huwa-l-Lāhu aḥad*, 107

Whoever visits them and greets them, until the Day of Resurrection, they definitely answer him, 52
Whoever wants to bask in Paradise let him keep to the congregation, 22
You have reached recognition so stick to it, 23
You must keep with the congregation. Beware of parting, 22
Your deeds are displayed to the dead, so if they see goodness, 44

www.ingramcontent.com/pod-product-compliance
Lightning Source LLC
Chambersburg PA
CBHW030527080526
44586CB00011B/353
* 9 7 8 1 9 3 0 4 0 9 2 7 9 *